BASEBALL BIOGRAPHIES FOR KIDS

D1052600

BASEBALL
BIOGRAPHIES
FOR KIDS

THE GREATEST PLAYERS
FROM THE 1960s TO TODAY

DEAN BURRELL

Illustrations by
BRENNA DAUGHERTY

ROCKRIDGE
PRESS

Copyright © 2020 by Rockridge Press, Emeryville, California

No part of this publication may be reproduced, stored in a retrieval system, or transmitted in any form or by any means, electronic, mechanical, photocopying, recording, scanning, or otherwise, except as permitted under Sections 107 or 108 of the 1976 United States Copyright Act, without the prior written permission of the Publisher. Requests to the Publisher for permission should be addressed to the Permissions Department, Rockridge Press, 6005 Shellmound Street, Suite 175, Emeryville, CA 94608.

Limit of Liability/Disclaimer of Warranty: The Publisher and the author make no representations or warranties with respect to the accuracy or completeness of the contents of this work and specifically disclaim all warranties, including without limitation warranties of fitness for a particular purpose. No warranty may be created or extended by sales or promotional materials. The advice and strategies contained herein may not be suitable for every situation. This work is sold with the understanding that the Publisher is not engaged in rendering medical, legal, or other professional advice or services. If professional assistance is required, the services of a competent professional person should be sought. Neither the Publisher nor the author shall be liable for damages arising herefrom. The fact that an individual, organization, or website is referred to in this work as a citation and/or potential source of further information does not mean that the author or the Publisher endorses the information the individual, organization, or website may provide or recommendations they/ it may make. Further, readers should be aware that websites listed in this work may have changed or disappeared between when this work was written and when it is read.

For general information on our other products and services or to obtain technical support, please contact our Customer Care Department within the United States at (866) 744-2665, or outside the United States at (510) 253-0500.

Rockridge Press publishes its books in a variety of electronic and print formats. Some content that appears in print may not be available in electronic books, and vice versa.

TRADEMARKS: Rockridge Press and the Rockridge Press logo are trademarks or registered trademarks of Callisto Media Inc. and/or its affiliates, in the United States and other countries, and may not be used without written permission. All other trademarks are the property of their respective owners. Rockridge Press is not associated with any product or vendor mentioned in this book.

Interior and Cover Designer: Eric Pratt
Art Producer: Sue Bischofberger
Editors: Nicky Montalvo and Mary Colgan
Production Editor: Mia Moran

Illustrations © Brenna Daugherty, 2019 · brennadaugherty.com

ISBN: Print 978-1-64152-933-4 | eBook 978-1-64152-934-1

R0

"Never allow the fear of striking out keep you from playing the game!"

—Babe Ruth

CONTENTS

INTRODUCTION *viii*

IMPORTANT STAT ACRONYMS *xii*

RIGHTY PITCHER
GREG MADDUX   1
Legendary Great **TOM SEAVER**   7
Spotlight **GREATEST PITCHING ROTATION**   8
Beating the Odds **MO'NE DAVIS**   11

LEFTY PITCHER
RANDY JOHNSON   12
Legendary Great **SANDY KOUFAX**   20
Honorable Mention **BEST RELIEF PITCHERS**   22
Beating the Odds **JIM ABBOTT**   23

CATCHER
IVÁN RODRÍGUEZ   24
Legendary Great **JOHNNY BENCH**   31
Players from Around the World **JAPAN**   34

FIRST BASE
DAVID ORTIZ   36
Legendary Great **LOU GEHRIG**   42
Beating the Odds **JUSTINE SIEGAL**   45

SECOND BASE
CRAIG BIGGIO   46
Legendary Great **JACKIE ROBINSON**   55
Honorable Mention **BEST SLUGGER**   56

THIRD BASE
"CHIPPER" JONES   58
Legendary Great **EDDIE MATHEWS**   65
Players from Around the World **DOMINICAN REPUBLIC** 66

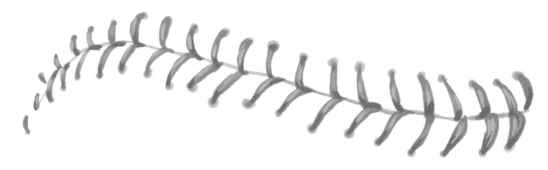

SHORTSTOP
CAL RIPKEN JR. 68
Legendary Great ERNIE BANKS 75
Beating the Odds JIM MECIR 77

LEFT FIELD
RICKEY HENDERSON 78
Legendary Great TED WILLIAMS 87
Spotlight GREATEST TEAM 88

CENTER FIELD
KEN GRIFFEY JR. 90
Legendary Great WILLIE MAYS 98
Players from Around the World CUBA 100

RIGHT FIELD
ICHIRO SUZUKI 102
Legendary Great HANK AARON 111
Beating the Odds CURTIS PRIDE 113

DESIGNATED HITTER
EDGAR MARTINEZ 114
Spotlight THE DESIGNATED HITTER RULE 122
Beating the Odds BO JACKSON 123
Honorable Mention FRANK THOMAS 125

MANAGER
TONY LA RUSSA 126
Legendary Great CONNIE MACK 133
Spotlight THE LONGEST GAME IN BASEBALL HISTORY 134
THE OLDEST MAJOR LEAGUE BASEBALL STADIUM 136

CREATE YOUR OWN STARTING LINEUP *138*
REFERENCES *140*
INDEX *148*

INTRODUCTION

I remember the first time I set foot inside a major league ballpark. I had recently moved to San Francisco, and a buddy of mine was eager to go see the San Francisco Giants. We took the bus to Candlestick Park, purchased tickets at the gate, and sat on the bleachers, taking it all in. There was something about the enormity of it all, from the perfectly groomed field to the players' pristine uniforms, that said, "*This* is baseball." I still get chills each time I enter a ballpark. The first thing I do is still head straight to the field.

My buddy and I went to a lot of Giants games, mostly because we enjoyed being at the ballpark. Seeing a player make a great play and then hearing the crowd react in person is simply electrifying. At first, I was content to marvel at individual accomplishments. A towering home run is remarkable to see, especially at the stadium. Over time, I began to see glimpses of strategy amid the spectacle. That's when the game's complexity began to unfold.

Years later, I started making the annual trek to spring training in Arizona. The months following the World Series were grueling. I would count the days until pitchers and catchers reported to the spring camps. "Pitchers & Catchers" should be marked on the calendar as a holiday, if you ask me. Seeing the prospects and veterans, and hearing about which young players were being "looked at," was so exciting.

The company I was with had a softball team that I would watch in the evenings. The fields weren't quite as perfectly groomed, but the games were fun. That was when I learned to keep score. I had seen fans keeping score in the stands at Candlestick Park, but never quite understood why. After all, that's what the scoreboard was there for, right? At the softball games, I was the scorekeeper—the one keeping track of the details. Keeping score changed how I saw the game. If you've never kept score, I encourage you to try it. I guarantee you'll see something about the game you haven't before. You'll likely have some great conversations with the fans nearby as you unravel tricky plays.

Every team in every sport has its stars, and baseball is no exception. Often, they're the reason that fans are drawn to a team. Like Cal Ripken Jr. in Baltimore. Or Ichiro Suzuki, considered by many in Japan to be a national hero. Go to a game, and you'll see fans wearing jerseys with their favorite player's name on the back. Now, what if you could assemble a team made up of your favorites? Whom would you choose for each position?

This book is my attempt at answering those questions. Following the rules of scoring, I organized this dream team by position number (1 = pitcher, 2 = catcher, 3 = first base, etc.), with a couple additions for the designated hitter and manager. The book also includes some runners-up for each position, because there are just too many outstanding players.

By and large, the book focuses on players from the past several decade and includes fun and interesting facts about them. Throughout its long history, baseball has undergone many changes that have had profound effects on the modern style of play. For example, in the late 1960s, Major League Baseball changed the height of the pitcher's mound when it saw that pitchers had an advantage that prevented batters from hitting the ball. Pitching statistics changed remarkably after that. The designated hitter (DH) is also a relatively recent addition, only appearing on the scene in the early 1970s.

Accordingly, I chose players who have retired in recent memory (from 2001 to 2009). You might hear them on the radio or see them at the ballpark. And if you're really lucky, you might even get an autograph or get to ask a few questions. Active players were excluded—maybe I'm superstitious. (Many players are! Cleveland Indian Yasiel Puig licks his bat for good luck.) But just in case, I'd rather not jinx anyone.

I've been fortunate enough to meet a handful of players throughout the years, and I'm always appreciative of the reminder that they're regular people, like you and me. I once ran into Oakland Athletics pitcher Vida Blue while getting lunch, and he proceeded to talk my ear off, proving that he genuinely appreciates meeting his fans. Admirable character traits like this also played a role in player selection in this book, because a great team isn't just about the statistics but also about who the players are beyond their achievements in sports. The 541 home runs David Ortiz hit by the end of his career may be remarkable, but so are the many ways in which he gives back to his communities in Boston and the Dominican Republic.

My hope for you with this book is that you learn a few things about these outstanding players and that you, too, come to understand that greatness isn't just about the skill a player brings to the game. Just as I learned to appreciate the game differently once I started to keep score, perhaps this book will allow you to understand greatness in a new way.

IMPORTANT STAT ACRONYMS

AB = At Bat. An at bat is a record of each time a batter takes a turn against a pitcher, with a couple of exceptions. The important thing here is that a player's number of at bats is used as the basis for several other statistics, such as batting average and slugging percentage. However, it must be noted that at bats are different from plate appearances. If a player walks, is hit by a pitch, or hits a sacrifice bunt or sacrifice fly ball, the plate appearance does not count as an at bat.

AVG = Batting Average. A player's batting average measures a batter's performance—number of hits—compared to his or her attempts or at bats. The AVG is expressed as a decimal. For example, let's say that for every 10 at bats a player has, he gets two hits. His AVG would be .200.

BB = Base on Balls, Walk, Intentional Walk. There are two kinds of walks—unintentional and intentional. In both cases, the pitcher has failed to throw strikes, and the batter is awarded first base.

CG = Complete Game. This is a statistic for pitchers, and it records any game where the pitcher remains on the mound for all innings, recording 27 outs.

ER = Earned Run. A run is earned by the batting team each time it scores without any assistance from the opposing defense. Let's say that there's a runner at second base, and the batter hits a fly ball deep to center field, well over the outfielder's head. The runner on second easily scores (while the outfielder chases the ball around the field). The run is earned. Now, let's say the fly ball lands in the outfielder's glove, but he accidentally drops it. This is considered an error, and the resulting run is now unearned.

ERA = Earned Run Average. A pitcher's ERA stands for the average number of *earned* runs given up by the pitcher over the course of a *nine-inning game*. But we need to take this apart a bit. First, we're talking about earned runs—runs scored when the defense hasn't made any errors. Second, nowadays pitchers rarely pitch nine innings. So, to calculate an ERA, you take the number of earned runs given up (let's say it's four runs), divide that by the number of innings pitched (let's say five), and then multiply that by nine (pretending that the pitcher lasted the full game, which he most certainly has not). His ERA for this game would be 7.2. The pitcher was then on pace to give up over seven runs.

G = Games Played. A pretty simple number, really. There are 162 regular-season games played by every team in the major league. As a player appears in more games, we get a better idea of his ability. A .300 batting average after just a handful of games is nice; a .300 average over the course of an entire season is one for the record books.

H = Hit. A hit is recorded any time a batter reaches base by hitting the ball. Well, almost. Remember that fly ball that popped out of the fielder's glove (the error)? Sorry, batter. No hit for you. You should've been out.

HR = Home Run. Ah, the holy grail. The outfielders watch helplessly as the ball flies into the stands and the runner rounds the bases.

IP = Innings Pitched. The number of innings a pitcher picks up as the season progresses. It's a measure of how durable a pitcher is.

L = Loss. A record of each time a pitcher loses the game. Compare with the number of wins.

OBP = On-base Percentage. The on-base percentage, or on-base average, is a measure of how frequently a batter reaches base. But it doesn't include instances where the runner reaches base because of the defense. So, if a fielder makes an error or chooses to throw out a runner already on base (scored as a fielder's choice), the batter's OBP remains unaffected. (The point here is that he should've been out.)

R = Run. Another term for each time a runner scores.

RBI = Runs Batted In. A batter records an RBI any time a run scores because of his hit. (By the way, a home run counts as an RBI.)

SO = Strikeout. Pitchers record a strikeout whenever a batter is called out at the plate. Batters can either swing at and miss the ball or just stand there as the ball crosses the strike zone.

SLG = Slugging Percentage. While the batting average measures a player's hits in relation to the number of at bats, the slugging percentage goes deeper. The SLG measures a player's ability to get extra-base hits. Basically, a high slugging percentage means that the batter is likely hitting doubles, triples, and home runs (not just singles).

W = Win. A record of each time a pitcher wins a game. Compare with the number of losses.

2B = Double. The batter safely reaches second base after hitting the ball. We can assume that the ball is hit deep into the outfield and, probably, the player is a fast runner. The outfielder cannot make an error, though, for the hit to be recorded as a double.

3B = Triple. As with a double, the batter safely reaches third base after hitting the ball. The ball is hit deep into the field, the player is fast, and no errors are made.

GREG MADDUX

RIGHTY PITCHER

31

GREG MADDUX

HEIGHT: 6'0" | WEIGHT: 170LB
BORN: APRIL 14, 1966
SAN ANGELO, TX

CAREER STATS

G	W	L	ERA	CG	IP
744	355	227	3.16	109	5,008.1
H	R	ER	HR	BB	SO
4,726	1,981	1,756	353	999	3,371

8X ALL-STAR
4X CY YOUNG AWARD WINNER
18X GOLD GLOVE

*"I would love to try to win another game.
Obviously, it's more fun when you win.
I'd rather try and not win than not try at all."*

1986–2008

1

While on the field, Greg Maddux studied his opponents' actions closely, applying what he learned to deliver his pitches with precision. Teammates said that he noticed even minor details, like where a batter placed his feet or how far he extended his arms when hitting. Maddux redefined the term "control" when it comes to pitching.

Maddux earned several Gold Glove and Cy Young Awards during his career for his excellent pitching. With Maddux in their corner, the Atlanta Braves gave up the fewest runs in the National League in 1993 and won their first-ever World Series in 1995. He was inducted into the Baseball Hall of Fame in 2014.

Gregory Alan Maddux was born on April 14, 1966, in San Angelo, Texas, to Dave and Linda Maddux. His father was a member of the US Air Force. He was stationed around both the United States and Europe during Maddux's childhood, and it was while living in Spain that Maddux discovered his love of baseball.

As a youngster, Maddux often played baseball with kids who were much older and bigger than he was. It was difficult for him to keep up, so his analytical mind began seeking out unique advantages. By paying attention and playing smart, he could compete against players of greater skill or athleticism.

In 1976, when Maddux was 10 years old, his family moved to Las Vegas. There, Maddux's older brother, Mike, who also played baseball, caught the attention of a former major league scout who offered instruction to promising youths. At their father's prompting, the scout also took a look at the younger Maddux and quickly saw the pitcher's potential. The scout encouraged him to try to keep batters off balance rather than overpowering them. This strategy fit well with Maddux's keen sense of observation.

His strategic approach to playing, paired with the scout's instruction, led Maddux to excel as a player at Valley High School. Upon graduation, Maddux immediately entered the baseball draft. He progressed through the minor leagues quickly and made his major league debut in 1986.

Maddux stood at less than six feet tall and weighed roughly 150 pounds when he graduated from high school, and he wasn't much bigger when he began playing for the Cubs in 1986. His manager mistook the young pitcher for the batboy when they first met. This kid clearly wasn't going to overpower the opposing batters, or so he thought. Though Maddux struggled during his first full season in the majors, his pitching improved greatly the following year. In 1988, his record was 18–8, with a 3.18 ERA. That season marked the beginning of a 17-year streak during which Maddux won 15 or more games.

BASEBALL BIOGRAPHIES FOR KIDS

Maddux established himself in 1989 with 19 game wins (19–12, 2.95 ERA). In addition, he was awarded the Gold Glove in 1990, 1991, and 1992. He also won the Cy Young Award—handed out annually to the best Major League Baseball pitchers—in 1992, when he posted a 20–11 record with a 2.18 ERA and an incredible 199 strikeouts.

The Atlanta Braves picked up Maddux in 1993. The team already had a dominant pitching staff in place. With the addition of Maddux, they gave up the fewest runs in the National League in 1993. He won his second and third consecutive Cy Young Awards in 1993 and 1994. After helping the Braves win their first-ever World Series in 1995, he won his fourth Cy Young Award.

FAST FACTS

- Maddux was nicknamed "Mad Dog" and "The Professor" because of his strategic approach to understanding other players' strengths and weaknesses.

- Maddux is the only MLB player to win 15 games during 17 consecutive seasons.

The Braves returned to the World Series in 1996. By this point, Maddux and the Braves had become a well-oiled machine. Maddux went 19–9 in both 1999 and 2000, and he regularly appeared in the All-Star Game. He remained with the Braves through 2003, pitching consistently before returning to the Chicago Cubs in February 2004. In August of that year, he won his 300th career game. In July of the following year, Maddux recorded his 3,000th win. But that year also brought him a 13–15 record, his first losing record since his first full season in the majors in 1987.

In the middle of 2006, he was traded to the Los Angeles Dodgers, who were looking to add pitching depth. Maddux did not disappoint his new team. He needed just 68 pitches to get through eight innings during his second game. By the end of this 18th season, he marked 15 or more wins, taking the Dodgers into the postseason. Unfortunately, the Dodgers were later swept by the New York Mets. Maddux ended his career in 2008, after brief stints with the San Diego Padres and again with the Dodgers.

Former teammates relied on Maddux's keen observations, which he shared willingly, to help them win games. He proved that you don't always need to overpower your opponents to win. You just need to play smart.

RUNNERS-UP

PEDRO MARTINEZ

Pedro Martinez debuted for the Los Angeles Dodgers when he was 20 years old, but made his name while pitching for the Boston Red Sox. Throughout an 18-year career, the right-hander won three Cy Young Awards and ranked 13th on the list of pitchers with 3,000 or more strikeouts. His foundation equips young aspiring players with job skills in case their baseball dreams don't pan out.

NOLAN RYAN

Nolan Ryan tops the strikeout leaders list with 5,714, more than 800 over the next highest (Randy Johnson, 4,875). Known as "the Ryan Express," he pitched until he was 46 years old. His fastball regularly topped 100 miles per hour, right up until he retired. Nolan's career consisted of more than baseball. He served in the Army Reserve and later authored books, owned businesses, and became engaged in political life.

BOB GIBSON

Bob Gibson, another member of the "3,000-strikeout club," played 17 seasons, all for the Saint Louis Cardinals. Despite a childhood marred by asthma and pneumonia, he became a truly dominant pitcher. Gibson holds the record for the lowest ERA (1.12) of any starting pitcher dating back to the early 1900s.

Legendary Great

TOM SEAVER

During their first seven years as a franchise, the New York Mets never had a winning season. In fact, the team lost at least 100 games during five of those years—not exactly a promising start for a new team. Enter Tom Seaver, a young pitcher who joined the team in 1967. Seaver pitched 18 complete games and had an ERA of 2.76 during his rookie season. He was also named the National League's Rookie of the Year. Two years later, Seaver's 25–7 record was instrumental in turning the team's luck around and guiding the Mets to their first-ever World Series trophy. The story of the 1969 "Miracle Mets" is legendary, and Seaver is at the heart of it.

Over the course of his career, Seaver won the Cy Young Award three times—the most of any Mets pitcher—and he was inducted into the Baseball Hall of Fame in 1992. Above his other accomplishments, he is most loved for transforming the Mets into formidable foes during the team's first decade and solidifying their place in Major League Baseball.

Often called "Tom Terrific" after a cartoon character who could transform himself into whatever he wished, Seaver lived up to the name. He went from high school baseball to the US Marine Corps Reserve to the major leagues and later into broadcasting and winemaking.

Spotlight

GREATEST PITCHING ROTATION

For seven straight years between 1993 and 1999, the Atlanta Braves pitching rotation rested firmly on the shoulders of Greg Maddux, Tom Glavine, and John Smoltz. Though the team had other notables rounding out the pitching squad, no trio of pitchers has been as dominant as Maddux,

Glavine, and Smoltz—neither before nor after. They took home five Cy Young Awards during those years, and to say they were competitive, both on and off the field, is an understatement.

On their off days, the three brought their competitiveness to the golf course. When the team traveled to Florida, the trio regularly sought out Tiger Woods to play against. They would team up as one to compete with Tiger, often placing bets on who would win. After Tiger beat them soundly in a 1997 game, he took the envelope containing the friendly wager and placed it in his golf bag. The next year, they all played again, but this time the pitchers won. Tiger reached into his bag, pulled out the very same envelope, and handed it back. "I figured you guys would get me back someday," he said.

The three had another notable thing in common: their penchant for giving back. The Maddux Foundation donates game tickets to nonprofits. Glavine worked with Operation Backpack, helping equip homeless children with school supplies and raising money for childhood cancer research. Smoltz, too, worked with more than one charity and received several awards for his charitable work.

Beating the Odds

MO'NE DAVIS

Mo'ne Davis rose to international fame during the 2014 Little League World Series, when she became the first girl to pitch a shutout and then win a Little League World Series game. At 13 years of age, she threw a curveball that left hitters shaking their heads in disbelief, and her fastball reached a speed of 70 miles per hour. That's the equivalent of a 93-mile-per-hour pitch on a full-size diamond.

It's an understatement to say that Davis is a natural. The first time she stepped onto the mound to pitch, the opposing players, and even some of their parents, mocked her. But when they saw her face the first batter, the smiles faded. As she later recounted, "[T]hey were all shocked, and we didn't really hear anything from that side of the field." She later became the first Little Leaguer ever featured on the cover of *Sports Illustrated*. Davis is a role model to all young athletes, and today, at 18 years old, she remains a strong proponent of young women in sports, redefining what it means to "throw like a girl."

RANDY JOHNSON

LEFTY PITCHER

12

51

RANDY JOHNSON

HEIGHT: 6'10" | WEIGHT: 225LB
BORN: SEPTEMBER 10, 1963
WALNUT CREEK, CA

CAREER STATS

G	W	L	ERA	CG	IP
618	303	166	3.29	100	4,135.1

H	R	ER	HR	BB	SO
3,346	1,703	1,513	411	1,497	4,875

10X ALL-STAR
5X CY YOUNG AWARD WINNER
2001 WORLD SERIES MVP

"Work hard and have patience."

1988-2009

13

With more than 4,800 strikeouts during his career and a history of pitching into late innings, Randy Johnson should make anyone's list of great pitchers. One of the tallest pitchers to take the mound, his reach made it seem like he was 10 feet closer to the plate. Johnson was also known for having the ability to focus intensely. He could shut out all distractions and concentrate only on the catcher's mitt. This focus defined who Johnson was, both on and off the field.

In June 2008, while playing for the Arizona Diamondbacks, Johnson reached 4,673 strikeouts. Only a year later, in June 2009, while playing with the San Francisco Giants, he won his 300th game. He was the 24th pitcher ever to do so and just the sixth left-hander.

Randall David Johnson was born on September 10, 1963, in Walnut Creek, California, to Carol Hannah and Rollen Charles "Bud" Johnson. His mother worked odd jobs and volunteered for local organizations, while his father served as a police officer and security guard in nearby Livermore. Johnson, who was one of five siblings, took an early interest in photography and sports.

Johnson attended Livermore High School, where he played both basketball and baseball. Standing at six feet and nine inches, he was also a promising and menacing pitcher. His fastball had already reached 90 miles per hour, easily over-powering his suburban opponents. It was common to see a line of scouts pointing radar guns behind the backstop when he was on the mound. But Johnson was still working on his control and often accidentally sent batters scurrying out of the box.

After completing high school in 1982, Johnson turned down an offer to join the Atlanta Braves. Instead, he chose to enroll at the University of Southern California (USC) with a full athletic scholarship to play baseball. While in school, Johnson studied photography, which became a lifelong passion. Johnson was remarkable as a pitcher during his three years at USC. However, his erratic command on the mound continued to plague him. Fortunately, his fast pitches caught the right people's eyes.

In 1985, the Montreal Expos drafted Johnson as their second-round pick. He made his Major League Baseball debut in September 1988. Johnson went 3–0 in four games at the end of 1988, but started the 1989 season with no wins. In May 1989, he was traded to the Seattle Mariners. He led the American League in walks during his first three seasons with the Mariners. He also led the league in hit batsmen in 1992 and 1993.

In 1992, he received a tip that would change everything. Johnson's pitches had him landing on the heel of his right foot, which caused his momentum to pull toward third base. A fellow pitcher suggested that he try landing on the ball of his foot so his momentum would align more with home plate. The adjustment worked almost immediately, and Johnson started consistently finding the strike zone. In a September 1992 game against the Texas Rangers, Johnson struck out 18 batters during eight innings. On the way to doing this, he threw 160 pitches, a number that hasn't been reached in a major league game since.

Pitching mechanics now sorted out, Johnson experienced many winning years throughout the next decade. In 1993, he had a 19–8 record, the first of six 300-plus strikeout seasons. In 1995, Johnson won 18 games, going 18–2, with a 2.48 ERA and 294 strikeouts. His record that year earned him his first Cy Young Award, making him the first Mariners pitcher to ever receive it.

The Houston Astros acquired Johnson in mid-1998. He posted a remarkable 10–1 record during 11 starts. Traded again in 1999, Johnson joined the Arizona Diamondbacks. The franchise was only in its second year, and this was arguably one of the best free-agent deals ever made.

Though the wins piled up, Johnson didn't pay much attention to the stats. His focus was always on the game and the next pitch. "When I was pitching, I had tunnel vision, and I was looking at the little glove that I was throwing my fastball to," he once said.

FAST FACTS

- While he was with the New York Yankees, Johnson pitched on Opening Day against the Boston Red Sox. It's rare for a newcomer to open the season for a team, but he was just that valuable to this team.

- Johnson won the National League's Cy Young Award every year for four years straight, starting in 1999.

- Johnson played in the major leagues for a whopping 22 seasons.

The New York Yankees acquired Johnson in 2005 with the hope that he would provide the final push the team needed to get into the postseason. Johnson rejoined the Diamondbacks in 2007. The next year, in June, he reached a strikeout number of 4,673, placing him in the number-two spot for all-time strikeout leaders. In June 2009, now with the San Francisco Giants, he won his 300th game. He retired from professional baseball in January 2010.

Johnson's single-minded focus helped him dominate the leagues. "I was extremely intense when I played. I just felt like I was wired that way," he admitted. That same focus made him a World Series co-MVP, got him named to the Mariners Hall of Fame, earned him numerous awards, and got him elected to the National Baseball Hall of Fame.

After Johnson left the game, he returned to his other passion, photography. Pitching and taking great photos both require singular focus for success, so it's no surprise that photography came naturally to him as well. He also applied that focus to raising more than $1 million for cystic fibrosis charities.

RUNNERS-UP

TOM GLAVINE

Tom Glavine, who in 2008 released a wine called "Cabernet Glavingnon" to raise money for childhood cancer research, is the only major league pitcher to start in more than 600 games (682). He is also the fifth left-handed pitcher to win 300 or more games.

ANDY PETTITTE

Andy Pettitte never had a year with a losing record during his 18-year career. He ranks first in strikeouts in New York Yankees history. Pettitte knew from the moment he first learned about the game that he wanted to make it his life's ambition, and his determination to realize his goal paid off.

Legendary Great

SANDY KOUFAX

Considered to be the greatest living Dodger, a drive to excel defines Sandy Koufax both on and off the field. On the mound, Koufax threw a dominant fastball, but he was known for his curveball. To batters, his curve was intense enough to put a damper on their game. In person, Koufax was extremely modest and crafty in his ability to side-step attention. His grandfather had taught him to guard his time, his most precious asset.

On the field, he was all grace and power. From 1961 to 1966, Koufax was an All-Star for six seasons, winning the National League's Most Valuable Player Award in 1963. He also won three Cy Young Awards and was the first major league pitcher to throw four no-hitters. But his career was cut short by debilitating arthritis in his throwing arm. The pain got so bad he couldn't straighten his left arm. So, at the age of 30, possibly the greatest pitcher the game has seen announced his retirement, ending a 12-year career.

Even after retiring, though, he always looked for ways to excel. When he golfed, he aimed to be good enough to win amateur tournaments. When he took up fishing, he moved to Idaho in pursuit of the best salmon streams. This drive for excellence seeped through every attempted undertaking. Despite staying out of the limelight in his retirement, he accepted baseball executive Joe Torre's invitation to join him on stage to speak about baseball as a way to raise money to help domestic abuse victims.

Honorable Mention

BEST RELIEF PITCHERS

MARIANO RIVERA AND TREVOR HOFFMAN

Since Major League Baseball names two best relievers—one for each league—we'll do the same: Mariano Rivera (American League) and Trevor Hoffman (National League). With a career ERA of 2.21 and a record 652 saves, Rivera is an easy pick. His signature pitch was the cut fastball, a pitch with such unbelievable movement that it left batters stunned, even though they knew it was coming. On the other side of the country, there was Hoffman, with a 2.87 ERA and 601 saves. Hoffman's signature pitch was a changeup. Remarkably, the pitch always arrived at the plate in the mid-70-miles-per-hour range.

Both Rivera and Hoffman are atop the list, in their respective leagues, for the most saves in a career. They made such an impact that the MLB named awards after them. Rivera, a devout Christian, has funded various church startups and supports education for underprivileged children through his charity, the Mariano Rivera

Foundation. Hoffman, who lost a kidney as an infant, would donate $200 to the National Kidney Foundation for every save made in a game. He also regularly pays for game tickets and meals for military service members and their families in honor of his dad, a former marine.

Beating the Odds

JIM ABBOTT

Born and raised in Michigan, Jim Abbott received multiple awards throughout his college career before joining the major leagues, where he pitched for 10 years. Drafted by the California Angels in 1989, Abbott went directly from the University of Michigan to the Angels starting rotation, completely skipping the minor leagues. His best season was in 1991, when he won 18 games and posted an ERA of 2.89.

Beyond his success as a pitcher, Abbott is best known for playing despite having no right hand. During games, Abbott wore a left-handed glove, which he rested on his right forearm as he threw. He would then quickly switch the glove to his left hand to field balls. In spite of this seeming limitation, Abbott was effective at throwing runners out at first base and even starting the occasional double play. His love of the game drove him to work hard, and his determination showed every day.

IVÁN RODRÍGUEZ

CATCHER

24

7

IVÁN RODRÍGUEZ

HEIGHT: 5'9" | WEIGHT: 205LB
NOVEMBER 27, 1971
MANATÍ, PUERTO RICO

CAREER STATS

G	AB	R	H	2B	3B
2,543	9,592	1,354	2,844	572	51
HR	RBI	BB	AVG	OBP	SLG
311	1,332	513	.296	.334	.464

14X ALL-STAR
13X GOLD GLOVE
7X SILVER SLUGGER

*"I don't play it for the money.
I play it because I love the game."*

1991–2011

25

As early as high school, people noticed that Iván Rodríguez had defined a direction for himself. A sense of purpose seemed to guide him. He had a level of maturity that set him apart from other kids his age. This showed most clearly in his work ethic. Rodríguez had a plan for his life, and to get there he learned all he could as he achieved his goals.

Though it's difficult to pick out just one moment of glory during Rodríguez's career, 1994 kicked off a wildly successful streak in his life. He batted .298, leading the American League in catchers. Throughout the rest of the 1990s, he led the Texas Rangers—and sometimes the league—in several categories, including batting average, hits, runs, doubles, and at bats by a catcher. In 1999, he was named the American League's Most Valuable Player.

Iván Rodríguez Torres was born in Manatí, Puerto Rico, on November 27, 1971, to José Rodríguez and Eva Torres. His father worked in construction, and his mother was a schoolteacher. Rodríguez tried both pitching and playing at third base before moving to catcher. Even at the age of seven or eight, his throwing arm was impressive.

Although Rodríguez had a job delivering flyers at a local mall in his early years, baseball was his passion. Growing up, his baseball idol was Johnny

Bench, the famed catcher for the Cincinnati Reds. He saw a lot of himself in Bench, which made him feel like he could succeed in baseball as well. "Watching [Bench] gave me some hope that I might have a shot," he said.

While in high school, Rodríguez was noticed by a big-league scout. Back then, the major league rules on what age a player had to be to get signed did not extend to Puerto Rico. When Rodríguez was signed by the Texas Rangers, he was just 16 years old. Rodríguez debuted in the minor leagues in 1989 at the age of 17. The next year, he was named the best catcher in the Florida State League. He led his team that season in RBIs (55). Despite being one of the youngest players, he rose quickly through the minor league system.

The Texas Rangers called him up to the majors in June 1991. Rodríguez was just 19 when he debuted for the Rangers. He was very nervous during his first game, but Benito Santiago, a well-known major league catcher from Puerto Rico to whom Rodríguez had reached out for pointers, had schooled him on what to expect at the major-league level. That night, he got his very first hit and drove in two runs. The following year (1992), Rodríguez was still the youngest player in the major leagues. He started in 112 games that year.

During the off-season, Rodríguez played ball in the Puerto Rico Baseball League to further develop his skills. "Pudge," as he was nicknamed, looked for every opportunity to hone his athletic skills. He was considered to be one of the best at throwing out runners trying to steal. But a good catcher does more than that. Catchers suggest what pitches to throw based on many factors, such as the number of balls and strikes as well as each pitcher's strengths and weaknesses. As Rodríguez gained more experience, he began working better with the pitchers.

FAST FACTS

- Rodríguez made it into the Texas Sports Hall of Fame in 2014.

- Following his retirement, Rodríguez became a postgame analyst for Fox Sports Southwest, combining his love of the game with his penchant for learning new things.

The early 2000s were a bit bumpy for Rodríguez due to injuries. He fractured his thumb, developed tendonitis in one knee, and suffered from a herniated disc in his back—all in the span of just two years. Concerned about the injuries and looking to cut costs, the Rangers were reluctant to give him a big contract extension. Rodríguez moved on and was picked up by the Florida Marlins in 2003.

Now a veteran player, Rodríguez brought leadership to a young Marlins team—so much so that the team went to the World Series his first year there and won the championship. Proving that his prior injuries were not an issue, he set team records for both RBIs and batting average.

In 2004, Rodríguez chose not to stay in Florida and was acquired by the Detroit Tigers. He won his tenth consecutive Gold Glove Award and his seventh Silver Slugger Award, which is given to the best offensive player at each position on the field, during his first year on the team. Long after his teammates had gone home after games, he was known to run laps and continue to exercise to stay on top of his game. This routine allowed him to avoid back surgery.

In the middle of the 2008 season, Rodríguez was traded to the New York Yankees, but he saw limited playing time. The next year, he joined the Houston Astros, then finished the year with a two-month stint with the Texas Rangers. After the 2009 season, Rodríguez joined the Washington Nationals, where he shared catching duties. In 2012, he announced his retirement.

Rodríguez holds the record for the most games played as a catcher. He credits his two-decades-long career to his ability to remain disciplined in the face of injuries and his desire to keep improving, both by pushing himself physically and by always looking to learn from others. It was this disciplined approach to the game he so loves that took him from the dirt field in which he grew up playing to the major leagues.

Rodríguez also became known for his desire to help the less fortunate. He created the Iván "Pudge" Rodríguez Foundation, which helps struggling families in Puerto Rico, Dallas, and Fort Worth.

RUNNERS-UP

MIKE PIAZZA

Mike Piazza holds the record for the most home runs by a catcher. In his first six seasons, he hit 30 or more each year, the most by any catcher in history. Although Piazza's main passion is baseball, it's not his only passion, as he has dabbled in both music and acting. "I always tell people, don't be afraid to step outside your comfort zone to do something exceptional," he said in an interview.

CARLTON FISK

Carlton Fisk played for 24 years, the most in history played by a catcher. He also holds the record for the longest game played by a catcher—eight hours and six minutes (25 innings). Fisk may be best remembered for making a dramatic home run during the sixth game of the 1975 World Series. He has been equally impactful outside of the field, through his service on the honorary board of the Cancer Support Center and his work raising money for children's charities.

Legendary Great

JOHNNY BENCH

Johnny Bench announced early in his life—*in elementary school*—that someday he would become a major league ballplayer. The determined boy quickly began perfecting his autograph. Bench's father urged him to consider catching, figuring that position would present the best chance of success. At age 17, Bench's pronouncement came to be. He was drafted by the Cincinnati Reds.

Considered by ESPN to be the greatest catcher in baseball history, Bench's career spanned 17 years, from 1967 through 1983. Bench earned

10 Gold Glove Awards, was named the National League's MVP twice (in 1970 and 1972), appeared in 14 All-Star Games, and was a vital contributor to back-to-back World Series wins in 1975 and 1976. He was inducted into the National Baseball Hall of Fame in 1989. But these ribbons barely do justice to his career. As former manager Sparky Anderson succinctly put it, "Don't compare any other catcher to Johnny Bench. It would be embarrassing."

Bench's ability to focus single-mindedly on whatever he wished to achieve not only earned him a remarkable career in baseball, but also helped him succeed in other areas of life. He was named valedictorian as a high school student, and following his baseball career, he dabbled in acting and professional golfing. He also published two books.

Players From Around the World

JAPAN

Baseball in Japan dates back almost as long as professional ball in the United States. An American teacher in Tokyo named Horace Wilson introduced the game in the early 1870s. Several years later, a Japanese engineer returning from the US brought the sport to his coworkers and formed the first organized team, the Shimbashi Athletic Club, in 1878. Throughout the next two decades, the game spread quickly to schools and universities.

In the early 1900s, Japanese teams began traveling to the US to hone their skills, and throughout the early twentieth century, American teams traveled to play the Japanese. Teams from several universities and the Negro Leagues made the trip, and even the New York Giants and Chicago White Sox traveled across the Pacific. It was no surprise that the touring Americans dominated their amateur opponents.

Then, in 1934, Japanese baseball made a huge leap forward. A touring team of American All-Stars led by Babe Ruth traveled to Japan for a series of exhibitions. The Japanese, in turn, formed a team of All-Stars of their own. Once again, the Americans prevailed, winning all 18 games, but instead of disbanding after the tour, the Japanese team stayed together and named themselves the Yomiuri Tokyo Giants. Professional baseball in Japan had begun.

By 1937, eight teams had joined the newly formed Japan Professional Baseball League. After World War II, in 1950, with the addition of more teams, the league split in half and renamed itself Nippon Professional Baseball. Throughout the 1950s and into the 1970s, the Yomiuri Giants dominated the opposition, winning 19 of 24 pennants. That reign came to an end in 1974 as the league became more competitive.

Teams like the Hiroshima Carp, the Hankyu Braves, and the Seibu Lions rose to prominence. The league also saw the rise of stars like Sadaharu Oh, who hit 868 home runs over his career, and Sachio Kinugasa, who broke Lou Gehrig's record for consecutive games played. Nowadays, the transfer fee structure between MLB and Nippon Professional Baseball makes it almost prohibitive for Japanese players to make it into the majors. Still, many have found success in the United States. Among them are Ichiro Suzuki, Hideo Nomo, Hideki Matsui, Yu Darvish, and Daisuke Matsuzaka.

DAVID ORTIZ

FIRST BASE

36

34

DAVID ORTIZ

HEIGHT: 6'3" | WEIGHT: 230LB
BORN: NOVEMBER 18, 1975
SANTO DOMINGO, D.R.

CAREER STATS

G	AB	R	H	2B	3B
2,408	8,640	1,419	2,472	632	19
HR	RBI	BB	AVG	OBP	SLG
541	1,768	1,319	.286	.380	.552

10X ALL-STAR
7X SILVER SLUGGER
WORLD SERIES MVP

*"It doesn't matter if we were down 3-0.
You've just got to keep the faith.
The game is not over until the last out."*

1997-2016

BASEBALL BIOGRAPHIES FOR KIDS

David Ortiz is as much known for his game as for his friendly and caring personality. Off the field, he was regularly present in the community. After visiting a children's hospital in 2005, Ortiz was so moved by what he saw that he started the David Ortiz Children's Fund. He wanted a way to provide ongoing medical support for children in both the Dominican Republic and New England.

Ortiz found his stride only after joining the Boston Red Sox. In 2007, Ortiz batted a career-best .332. He led the Red Sox to the postseason and a World Series win over the Colorado Rockies. This was his second time leading the team to the World Series.

David Américo Ortiz Arias was born in Santo Domingo, in the Dominican Republic, on November 18, 1975. His parents were Enrique Ortiz and Angela Rosa Arias. His father, who had played professional and semiprofessional ball, introduced Ortiz to the game. Ortiz shared his dad's passion for baseball, attending games whenever he could.

Ortiz attended Estudia Espaillat High School in the Dominican Republic, where he starred as both a basketball and baseball player. His parents divorced while he was in high school. Yet, the family remained tightly knit, and his father was around all the time. Just days after his 17th birthday in 1992, Ortiz was signed by the Seattle Mariners. He debuted in the minor league in 1994, and by the next year, he was batting well over .300. He quickly established himself as one of the ball club's best hitting prospects.

FAST FACTS

- While playing for the Boston Red Sox, Ortiz was given his famous nickname "Big Papi" because he had a habit of referring to others as "papi," a term of endearment in Latinx communities.

- In 2004, Ortiz led the Red Sox to their first World Series win in 86 years, and it was not his last time leading the team to the World Series.

After being traded to the Minnesota Twins in 1996 in a roster shuffle, Ortiz appeared in his first major league game in the last month of the 1997 season. He earned the call-up after having an outstanding showing in the Twins minor league system, batting .317 with 31 home runs.

The 2001 season was marked by injury—Ortiz broke his wrist—but his home-run hitting at the end of the season demonstrated his potential.

Although he finished the 2002 season batting .272 with 20 home runs and had a clutch performance in the playoffs, the Twins decided to release him. A stroke of luck led Ortiz to sign with the Boston Red Sox in 2003. He was out to dinner with his longtime friend, Pedro Martinez (star pitcher for the Red Sox), after leaving the Twins. When Pedro learned that Ortiz was available, he jumped up from the table and phoned his team. Boston needed a first baseman, and Pedro had just the man for the job.

Ortiz flourished in Boston, and his career finally took off in 2003. He finished his first year there with a .288 batting average and 31 home runs. And in his first five years in Boston, Ortiz hit 208 home runs and drove in 642 RBIs. In 2004, Ortiz hit his 100th career home run and was named to the All-Star team for the first time. He continued his success in 2005, batting .300 with 47 home runs.

In 2010, his home runs (32) and RBIs (102) were near the top in the American League. Ortiz surged ahead in 2011. He batted .309 that year, with 29 home runs. Injury plagued him during the 2012 season. He played in only 90 of 162 games. But his performance in 2013 was outstanding. He batted .309 with 30 home runs. The Red Sox won the World Series that year, and Ortiz earned the Most Valuable Player Award.

Ortiz closed out his career in 2016 on top of his game. He batted .315, and he hit 38 home runs, the most in a season since 2006. After a 14-year career with the Red Sox, he was voted by the fans as one of the four greatest players in Boston Red Sox history. However, Ortiz made as much of an impact off the field as he did on it.

Ortiz was a model in his devotion to the community and to his family. In 2008 he received UNICEF's Children's Champion Award, which is given to people who work to save children who are suffering from illnesses with preventable causes. At the end of the 2010 season, he received the Roberto Clemente Award for his commitment to the community and his work with the David Ortiz Children's Fund.

RUNNERS-UP

WILLIE MCCOVEY

Willie McCovey was called "the scariest hitter in baseball" by Bob Gibson, a Hall of Fame pitcher. Over a 22-year career, he hit 18 grand slams, the most by any National League player. The same work ethic that prompted him to get a job at the early age of 12 was responsible for his rise to baseball fame.

JEFF BAGWELL

Jeff Bagwell played his entire career for the Houston Astros and was one of the famed "Killer B's" (along with Craig Biggio, Sean Berry, and Derek Bell) from the late 1990s. He holds Astros career records for RBIs, walks, and home runs. Bagwell, who was honored by his high school for his character and generosity, found ways to give back to the sport after a shoulder injury forced him into retirement by accepting coaching gigs and other special assignments with the Astros.

Legendary Great

LOU GEHRIG

Some players in the history of baseball are so synonymous with the game that their names are tossed around as though everyone just knows how great the players were. It's assumed we don't need to recount their feats because it feels like common knowledge. Lou Gehrig is one of those players.

Gehrig played first base for the New York Yankees for 17 years, from 1923 to 1939. He had the misfortune of playing in the shadows of Babe Ruth and Joe DiMaggio, two other legends of the game. Nonetheless, Gehrig put up such impressive numbers that he's rightfully considered a legend.

First, there's his consecutive game streak of 2,130 (a record that remained intact until Cal Ripken Jr. beat it in 1995). This feat alone earned him the nickname "Iron Horse" because he could play through tremendous pain. Having grown up in a poor family, he was motivated to work as hard as he could, and one of the first things he did upon signing his first professional contract was help his parents move to the suburbs.

Then there's the list of firsts. He was the first baseman in the first All-Star Game, the first player to have his number retired, the first to hit 20-plus grand slams, the first in the American League to hit four home runs in a game, and the first athlete to have his photo on a box of Wheaties cereal. Gehrig's record for grand slams remains unbeaten, and his record for home runs by a first baseman lasted longer than 50 years. Gehrig set the standard for baseball achievement toward which players today continue to strive.

Gehrig stopped playing after being diagnosed with amyotrophic lateral sclerosis (ALS), which prevents nerve cells from working with the muscles in the body. He used his retirement to create awareness of the condition, which is now often called Lou Gehrig's disease. Toward the end of his life, he became dedicated to helping troubled youths in his community.

Beating the Odds

JUSTINE SIEGAL

Like many, Justine Siegal spent her afternoons playing baseball with the neighborhood kids. But when a coach told her that girls are only supposed to play softball, her mind was made up: She would pursue the game she loved and become a baseball coach. That dream was first realized in 2002, when she coached an all-girls youth team. She became the first to compete in a national tournament for boys.

Siegal went on to coach for the Springfield College baseball team in Massachusetts, as the only woman coach at the collegiate level, and then the Brockton Rox, a former professional baseball franchise. In 2011, Siegal threw batting practice during spring training for the Cleveland Indians, becoming the first woman to do so. She threw BP for five more MLB teams. Finally, in 2015, Siegal became the first female coach in MLB history when the Oakland Athletics hired her as a guest instructor for the team's fall instructional league.

Currently, Siegal runs Baseball for All, a nonprofit organization that works toward gender equity in baseball. Most recently, she became a coach for the Fukushima Hopes in the Japanese minor league.

CRAIG BIGGIO

SECOND BASE

46

7

CRAIG BIGGIO

HEIGHT: 5'11" | WEIGHT: 185LB
BORN: DECEMBER 14, 1965
SMITHTOWN, NY

CAREER STATS

G	AB	R	H	2B	3B
2,850	10,876	1,844	3,060	668	55

HR	RBI	BB	AVG	OBP	SLG
291	1,175	1,160	.281	.363	.433

7X ALL-STAR
4X GOLD GLOVE
5X SILVER SLUGGER

"In baseball, tomorrow is not guaranteed, and I tried to play every game as if it was going to be my last."

1998-2007

47

Early in his life, Craig Biggio's dad gave him some advice that he would remember forever: Finish what you start. No matter what the circumstances are, follow through with the task you've taken on. For this reason, Biggio readily focused on the different roles his team, the Houston Astros, asked him to take on during his entire career. The different positions he played didn't always come easily. But he never gave up and worked hard to master each one.

Biggio always rose to the challenge. His offense and defense really jumped in 1993. That season, he batted .287, with 175 hits and 21 home runs, his highest total so far. He had become a reliable leadoff batter who hit for power. In 1994 and 1995, Biggio won both the Gold Glove and Silver Slugger Award.

Craig Alan Biggio was born on December 14, 1965, in Smithtown, New York, on Long Island, to Johnna and Gordon. As Biggio was growing up, his father worked long hours—nights and weekends—as an air-traffic controller. Despite the long hours, Gordon made time to teach his son baseball and encouraged him to be a catcher.

Biggio attended Kings Park High School, where he played both baseball and football. He was a star running back and seemed destined for a career in professional football. He was even prepared to quit the baseball team until his dad took him aside and reminded him that he had to finish what he started and not just give it up.

During his high school years, Biggio befriended a young neighbor who was struggling with leukemia. He was so impressed by the boy's positive spirit that he applied the same spirit to his approach of the game. It fit perfectly with his father's teaching to keep at it no matter what. Biggio decided to pursue baseball when he graduated from high school, and he accepted a scholarship to Seton Hall University.

At the end of his junior year in college, the Houston Astros chose Biggio in the first round of the 1987 major league draft. He signed immediately. He was later called up to the major league team in mid-1988. The team was in desperate need of a backup catcher. Starting with the 1989 season, Biggio was tapped to be the team's catcher going forward. He proved himself to be a fast runner with good base-stealing skills. In his first full year, he batted well and won his first Silver Slugger Award. Looking to preserve his base-running abilities (catching is very hard on a player's legs), the Astros also tried him in the outfield.

In 1992, the Astros manager suggested that Biggio move from catcher to second base. He had to learn to play a whole new position quickly. Biggio practiced from dawn to dusk during that spring training.

Biggio recorded his best season ever in 1997. He batted .325 with 210 hits, including 20 home runs. He had 50 doubles and 51 stolen bases in 1998, making him just the second major league player ever to reach 50 in each of those categories in the same season. In 1999, he hit 56 doubles, a career high.

Biggio's career began to take a downhill turn in 2000. It was the first year of his career that he landed on the disabled list. He missed the last two months of the season because of a knee injury. He rebounded in 2001, batting .292, but his performance slipped again in 2002, and he batted .253, a career low.

The Astros asked Biggio to move to center field in 2003. This was the second time the team asked him to try a new position. In 2004, the team yet again asked him to change positions, this time to left field. He took the moves in stride and readily embraced the extra work he needed to do to perform well in each position. Biggio retook second base in 2005, a move that finally felt comfortable for him. He retired at the end of the 2007 season.

At the end of his career, Biggio was formally recognized for his efforts—he won both the Hutch Award in 2005 and the Roberto Clemente Award in 2007. The Hutch Award recognizes players who persevere no matter how great the odds. The Clemente Award honors players for their sportsmanship, community involvement, and team commitment.

In 2004, *Sporting News* magazine named him one of the Good Guys of the game. Good Guys make notable contributions to the community off the field. As early as high school, Biggio made a commitment to support local charity. Throughout his playing days and afterward, he generously gave to the Sunshine Kids Foundation, a Houston-based organization dedicated to supporting children with cancer.

FAST FACTS

- Biggio's performance his first year in the minor leagues was so good (he batted .375) that he was invited to the Astros spring training camp.

- When the Astros asked Biggio to move to center field, he began running up to five miles daily to build up his stamina.

- Biggio hit a career high of 26 home runs in 2005, the same year he reached his 1,000th RBI. In 2007, he achieved his last significant milestone, his 3,000th hit.

RUNNERS-UP

ROBERTO ALOMAR

Roberto Alomar won the most Gold Glove Awards (10) ever by a second baseman. He was elected into four different baseball halls of fame: Canadian, Caribbean, Latino, and National. The son of a major leaguer, Alomar knew very early on that he wanted to continue his dad's legacy and make him proud.

ROD CAREW

Rod Carew was selected for the All-Star Game 18 times over his 19-year career. He was voted the Rookie of the Year his first year playing and the American League's Most Valuable Player a decade later. Carew, a US Marine Corps Reserve combat engineer, credited the military for teaching him the discipline he needed to succeed in the major leagues.

JOE MORGAN

Joe Morgan regularly led the league in on-base percentage while playing for the Cincinnati Reds. He was a member of the Reds "Big Red Machine" and won back-to-back Most Valuable Player Awards in 1975 and 1976. He stood up against injustice by successfully suing the Los Angeles Police Department after being wrongly arrested while at the Los Angeles International Airport in 1991. He also is on the board of the Baseball Assistance Team, a nonprofit that helps players experiencing financial hardship.

Legendary Great

JACKIE ROBINSON

Jackie Robinson was 28 years old when he ran onto the field for the Brooklyn Dodgers in 1947, becoming the first black player in the modern era of Major League Baseball, post-1900. In his rookie season, he played in 151 games, scored 125 runs, batted .297, and won the inaugural Rookie of the Year Award. By season's end, Robinson had become a fan favorite, both for his aggressive style of play and for crossing baseball's color line. Over the course of his 10-year career, Robinson had a career batting average of .311, was named the National League's MVP in 1949, and helped the Dodgers win six pennants.

When Dodgers general manager Branch Rickey first recruited Robinson, he asked that the player not respond to the abuse he was likely to face. Right from the first day he took the field, Robinson had to endure racial taunts from other players, including some of his own teammates. Off the field, he even received death threats in the mail. But Robinson stayed true to his promise of not reacting, and his demeanor paved the way for the nonviolence that would become the hallmark of the civil rights movement a decade later.

Honorable Mention

BEST SLUGGER

BABE RUTH

The all-time leader in slugging average is Babe Ruth (.690 SLG). He is directly followed by Ted Williams (.634) and Lou Gehrig (.632). A player's slugging average is a complicated formula that represents the average number of bases a player reaches per at bat, giving higher "weight" for more bases reached. A home run, for instance, counts higher than a single in the calculation. But, let's say that a batter hits a tremendous number of singles. His SLG will still be quite high, but we would be hard-pressed to say he hit for power. We're forced down the never-ending path of stats like extra-base hits (XBH), home runs (HR), on-base percentage (OBP), on-base plus slugging (OPS), and so on. We even hear about exit velocity and launch angle. What are we to do? Let's just leave it at, "the all-time leader in slugging average is Babe Ruth."

Ruth was sent to live at a reformatory as a youngster because of persistent bad behavior. However, he found a mentor there who encouraged him to apply himself to baseball. After gaining baseball fame, Ruth made it a point to repay the kindness, guidance, and encouragement he had received. He would visit orphanages, schools, and hospitals, donating generously to such institutions. He also gave to his old reformatory and even bought his old mentor a Cadillac.

"CHIPPER" JONES

THIRD BASE

58

10

"CHIPPER" JONES

HEIGHT: 6'4" | WEIGHT: 210LB
BORN: APRIL 24, 1972
DELAND, FL

CAREER STATS

G	AB	R	H	2B	3B
2,499	8,984	1,619	2,726	549	38

HR	RBI	BB	AVG	OBP	SLG
468	1,623	1,512	.303	.401	.529

8X ALL-STAR
2X SILVER SLUGGER
MVP AWARD

"I think baseball has such a way of humbling you. You can go 20-for-20, and before you know it, you're going to go through a 0-for-30."

1993-2012

Larry "Chipper" Jones is at the top of the list of all-time best switch-hitters ever to play baseball. He is the only switch-hitter in Major League Baseball history to hit above .300 from both sides of the plate. Hitting that well is remarkable for any player. Beyond all the stats and records broken, however, Jones is a guy who is loyal to his roots, including the team that gave him his first chance.

Jones played exclusively for the Atlanta Braves his entire career. In 2011, toward the end of his run, he recorded his 2,500th hit, 500th double, and 1,500th RBI, all in the month of April. He hit his 450th home run four months later.

Larry Wayne Jones Jr. was born on April 24, 1972, in DeLand, Florida, to Larry Sr. and Lynne Jones. His father taught mathematics at nearby Taylor High School, and his mother was a professional horseback rider. Because Larry Sr. played baseball in college, he also coached the high school team. The Joneses lived on a 10-acre farm outside a very small town.

When Jones was a child, people used to playfully comment that he looked so much like his dad that he was a "chip off the old block." The nickname stuck. Jones learned to play baseball from his dad. The two of them would play one-on-one games in the backyard for hours, pretending they were like the baseball stars of the day. By the time

Jones was in junior high, he was good enough to play on the varsity team.

For tenth grade, Jones switched to a private high school in a city about 100 miles away. His parents thought the local school wasn't challenging him enough. Jones considered himself to be a country boy, however, and he was immediately overwhelmed and homesick. Worse, his old friends looked at him like he was a traitor for leaving, and he would remember this throughout his entire baseball career.

He focused his extracurricular energy on baseball. By his senior year, professional scouts began to show up at his baseball games. He was named the Florida State Player of the Year, batting .488 as a shortstop. He also had a winning season as a pitcher.

The Atlanta Braves signed Jones right after he graduated from high school in 1990. Even though he could have made more money signing with another team, he was happy to be in Atlanta. "I'm a Southern kid, and I wanted to play in a Southern town where I felt comfortable," he said years later.

He entered the minor league in 1991 and batted .326 his first year. He moved up steadily over the next two years. The Atlanta Braves called him up to the big leagues in September 1993 as a backup shortstop. The Braves were on their way to the postseason and needed all the help they could get.

Jones stayed with the team for the 1994 season, but his season ended abruptly when he was injured. His major league debut came in April 1995 during a home game against the San Francisco Giants. He scored three runs in his first game. After a solid rookie year, Jones signed a four-year contract to stay with the Braves. During the 1996 season, he hit 30 home runs, batting .309. He was also selected for his first All-Star Game that season.

Jones performed well during both 1997 (batting .295) and 1998 (batting .313). The next year saw him at the top of his game. He batted .319, with 181 hits and 45 home runs, a career high. His performance earned him the National League's Most Valuable Player Award as well as the Silver Slugger Award.

Loyal to his team, Jones signed a contract extension with the Braves before starting the 2000 season. As with his earlier signings, he had no interest in other offers or other teams. In fact, when his agent tried to get him to look at other options, Jones fired him. He wasn't leaving Atlanta. Jones stayed at the top of his game throughout the remainder of the decade, never leaving his team until his retirement. He reluctantly retired at the end of the 2012 season after years of persistent knee problems.

Having spent 19 years with the same team, Jones developed a fan base that was as loyal to him as he had remained to the team. "I've been good to the Braves, but they've been better to me," he said toward the end of his playing days. Perhaps his father recounts it best: "Once he [signed with the Braves] he said, 'You know what, Dad? This is home.'" Always loyal to his team, he returned in 2016 as a team advisor.

FAST FACTS

- In 1995, the same year of Jones's major league debut, the Braves went to the World Series, and he received a World Series ring after defeating the Cleveland Indians.

- Jones made his 2,000th career hit in June 2007 and got his 372nd home run just a month later, making Braves history.

- Jones earned the National League's batting title after ending 2008 with a .364 batting average.

RUNNERS-UP

ADRIAN BELTRE

Adrian Beltre won the Gold Glove Award at third base five times. In addition, he won the rare Platinum Glove Award (for best defense in the entire league) twice. Beltre, who is from the Dominican Republic, has been involved with the I Love Baseball program, which works in his home country to equip young aspiring players to pursue their education, as well as with the Baseball Tomorrow Fund, which promotes youth participation in the sport.

MIKE SCHMIDT

Mike Schmidt is possibly considered the greatest third baseman. Over an 18-year career with the Philadelphia Phillies, he led the National League in home runs eight times, and he won the Gold Glove Award 10 times. Schmidt has sponsored an annual fishing tournament in the Bahamas and released a wine called Mike Schmidt 548 Zinfandel (in homage to the 548 home runs of his career) in support of cystic fibrosis research.

Legendary Great

EDDIE MATHEWS

Third baseman Eddie Mathews played 14 years of his 17-year career with the Braves and is the only player to have been with the team in all three cities they called home—Boston, Milwaukee, and Atlanta. Upon joining the team in the early 1950s, the Braves formed an identity that they've kept ever since. They were a team built on home-run power and veteran pitching. That was a reputation Matthews did his part to uphold.

In 1953, Mathews set the record for the most home runs by a third baseman (47) and is the only third baseman with 500 homers. Mathews was a pull hitter with power, so much so that opposing teams would employ what they called the "Mathews shift," in which the second baseman would move to his left and the shortstop would move to second base.

He attributed his pull hitting abilities to his mother. When he was young, he and his parents would play ball, and his mother would pitch. During his Hall of Fame induction speech, Mathews said, "Every time I hit a ball back through the middle, close to my mother, I got an additional chore to do, so my mother was instrumental in making me a pull hitter."

Players From Around the World

DOMINICAN REPUBLIC

Baseball was first introduced to the Caribbean islands in the mid-1800s by American sailors in Cuba. When the Ten Years' War for Cuban independence led to chaos in the country, many Cubans fled to the nearby islands, including the Dominican Republic, and the game of baseball came with them. The Dominicans took to the game quickly, and soon teams formed and tournaments were being held all over the island.

Dictator Rafael Trujillo solidified baseball's presence there in the 1930s and 1940s when he encouraged the sugar refineries to create teams for the laborers. Over the years, the level of play increased in both intensity and popularity. In 1937, stars from the American Negro League and well-known players from around Latin America were signed by Dominican teams, bringing even greater professionalism to the sport there. Unfortunately, the expensive contracts weren't sustainable. But the foundation had been laid, and the game continued to flourish.

With the creation of the Dominican League in 1951, baseball soared in popularity. The Dominican League started as a summer league, but switched to a winter schedule several years later to attract major league players who were in their off-season. The first Dominican to make it to the majors was Osvaldo Virgil Sr., who debuted for the New York Giants in 1956. Felipe Alou followed two years later, debuting with the Giants. More than 750 players from the Dominican Republic have joined the US major league since then.

Today, about a quarter of the players in Major League Baseball are born outside the US, and of those, the majority come from the Dominican Republic. Because of this, the Dominican Republic has become the dominant training center for young players from all over Central America and even South America. Each of the 30 major league teams has a training facility there. Baseball is such a way of life on the island that kids can regularly be seen playing on the streets, even if they don't have a proper bat or baseball. Many of baseball's greats—Pedro Martinez, David Ortiz, Vladimir Guerrero, Albert Pujols—continue to give back to their home country by helping build schools, churches, housing, and, of course, baseball fields on the island.

CAL RIPKEN JR.

SHORTSTOP

68

8

CAL RIPKEN JR.

HEIGHT: 6'4" | WEIGHT: 200LB
BORN: AUGUST 24, 1960
HAVRE DE GRACE, MD

CAREER STATS

G	AB	R	H	2B	3B
3,001	11,551	1,647	3,184	603	44

HR	RBI	BB	AVG	OBP	SLG
431	1,695	1,129	.276	.340	.447

19X ALL-STAR
2X GOLD GLOVE
8X SILVER SLUGGER

"As long as I can compete, I won't quit. Reaching three thousand [hits] is not the finish line as long as I can contribute."

1981-2001

Cal Ripken Jr. spent his entire major league career playing for the Baltimore Orioles. It was something of a family tradition, as his father had played for them as well. In fact, by the age of 12, Ripken was taking infield practice with his father's team. It's no surprise then that he grew up to join the team that had become like a second family to him.

The high point of Ripken's career came on September 6, 1995, when he passed Lou Gehrig's 56-year-old record for most consecutive games played (2,130). The Orioles were playing the California Angels in Baltimore. When the game became official at the end of the fifth inning, Ripken was treated to a 22-minute standing ovation.

Born on August 24, 1960, in Maryland to Cal Sr. and Violet, Calvin Edwin Ripken grew up traveling around the United States. His father was a minor league player and a coach in the Orioles organization. Before he was even a teenager, Ripken was destined to be a baseball player. Ripken's father was a coach and mentor to many, including his son. He told his son, "Do your best," and, "Take one day at a time," early on.

Though Ripken had started out in Little League as a catcher, he switched to second base when he entered high school in Aberdeen, Maryland. He was five feet, seven inches tall and weighed just 128 pounds. In his sophomore year, Ripken moved to shortstop and proved to be both a strong fielder and a team-leading hitter. It didn't hurt that by the age of 16, he was taking batting practice with the major league Orioles. The Aberdeen Eagles needed pitching, so Ripken took the mound in his junior year even though he was still playing the infield. His success continued into his senior year, where he struck out 100 batters and batted .492.

The Baltimore Orioles drafted Ripken in 1978 and put him at shortstop right from the beginning. In 1981, he played for the triple-A Rochester Red Wings. There, he hit 233 home runs and batted .288 as a third baseman. During this season, Ripken was involved in the longest professional baseball game in major league history. The Red Wings played the Pawtucket Red Sox in April of that year, and the total game time spanned three days. Ripken played all 33 innings—a sign of his stamina on the field.

The Orioles called Ripken up to the majors in August 1981 as a backup infielder. In early 1982, they made him their full-time third baseman. Ripken won the American League's Rookie of the Year Award. He also missed just three games that season, the last on May 29. This would be the last game he missed until 1998.

Ripken moved to shortstop in the middle of 1982, and at first, the critics were unsure that he could play the position well. But 1983 proved to be one of the best years in Ripken's career.

Along with the consecutive games streak, Ripken had been amassing consecutive innings. That innings streak came to an end in 1987, however. Up until mid-September, he had played 8,264 innings without a break. The manager worried that the streak had become something of a burden. Finally, he pulled Ripken from a game. "I had to do it sometime," he simply stated afterward. The manager was Ripken's dad, Cal Sr.

Ripken's offense surged in 1991. He won his second American League MVP Award and his first Gold Glove, earned the All-Star Game MVP (he also won the Home Run Derby, the home-run hitting contest held the day before the All-Star Game), won the Silver Slugger Award, and was named Player of the Year by both the Associated Press and *Sporting News*. The last time a player accumulated this many awards was in 1962.

"Rip," as he was sometimes called, was on a roll of consecutive games played and by this point was well on his way to surpassing Lou Gehrig's record. Ripken chose to end his streak in 1998, and on September 20, a rookie started in Ripken's place. Ripken wanted to end the streak on his own terms with no question about his abilities.

Ripken recorded the highest batting average of his career in 1999 (.340), and he hit the 400th home run of his career that September. The following year he recorded his 3,000th hit.

After retiring in 2001, Ripken followed in his dad's teaching footsteps. With his brother, Billy (also a former major leaguer), he started the Cal Ripken Sr. Foundation. The organization targets at-risk youth, teaching them the values and positive attitude that Cal Sr. had passed on to his sons.

FAST FACTS

- Ripken's brother, Billy, also played for the Orioles, marking the first time a father has managed two sons on the same team in baseball history. They played 663 games together.

- As a young player in 1983, Ripken led the majors in the number of hits and doubles, and he led the American League in runs scored. At 23, he was named the American League's Most Valuable Player.

- At 2,632 consecutive games, Ripken surpassed Gehrig's record by a whopping 502 games.

RUNNERS-UP

ALEX RODRIGUEZ

Alex Rodriguez holds a major league record with 25 career grand slams. He won the American League's Most Valuable Player Award three times during his career. He also donated $3.9 million to the University of Miami for renovations to the school's baseball stadium, which was renamed the Alex Rodriguez Park at Mark Light Field.

OZZIE SMITH

Ozzie Smith was nicknamed "The Wizard of Oz" for his defensive magic. He won an incredible 13 consecutive Gold Gloves. He is probably most well known for the signature backflip he made when he took his position at the start of each game. After his playing career, he launched a youth sports academy.

OMAR VIZQUEL

Omar Vizquel holds the record for the most games played at shortstop and for the most double plays turned in the major leagues. He played for 24 years. The Venezuela native helped raise more than $500,000 for relief efforts following a

1999 mudslide in his country that left thousands dead. That was only one of his charitable endeavors, as community service has been a big part of his personal life.

Legendary Great

ERNIE BANKS

"Work? I never worked a day in my life. I always loved what I was doing, had a passion for it." Ernie Banks so thoroughly enjoyed playing baseball that even his baseball cards reflected his infectious smile. Nicknamed "Mr. Cub" because of his joyful presence, Banks embodied all that is good about the game. He joined the Chicago Cubs when he was 22 after playing several years for the Kansas City Monarchs in the Negro Leagues.

He was the first African American to play for the Cubs and played his entire 19-year career with the team. Banks was the first Cubs player to win a Gold Glove at shortstop. He won back-to-back MVP Awards in 1958 and 1959 and was the first player in MLB history to hit five grand slams in a single season. Throughout his career, Banks played 2,000-plus games, but never once appeared in the postseason. In 1967, he won the Lou Gehrig Memorial Award, which is given to players who make exemplary philanthropic contributions to their community.

Beating the Odds

JIM MECIR

Jim Mecir pitched for 11 seasons in the majors, from 1995 to 2005, for five different teams. His story is remarkable because he was born with a clubfoot. Though several surgeries during his childhood enabled Mecir to walk, his right leg was forever one inch shorter than his left, and his right calf was half its normal size. He overcame these obstacles and led a notable career as a major leaguer.

He played for the New York Yankees in 1996 and 1997 and was part of the 1996 World Series–winning team. His five-year stint with the Oakland Athletics later in his career earned him prominent mention in the book *Moneyball* by Michael Lewis. In 2003, he was presented with the Tony Conigliaro Award, given annually to an MLB player who best over-came an obstacle. He was inducted into the New York Baseball Hall of Fame in 2016.

RICKEY HENDERSON

LEFT FIELD

78

24

RICKEY HENDERSON

HEIGHT: 5'10" | WEIGHT: 180LB
BORN: DECEMBER 25, 1958
CHICAGO, IL

CAREER STATS

G	AB	R	H	2B	3B
3,081	10,961	2,295	3,055	510	66

HR	RBI	BB	AVG	OBP	SLG
297	1,115	2,190	.279	.401	.419

10X ALL-STAR
GOLD GLOVE
3X SILVER SLUGGER

*"If my uniform doesn't get dirty,
I haven't done anything in the baseball game."*

1979-2003

Rickey Henderson was possibly the greatest lead-off hitter in baseball history. He scored more runs and stole more bases than any other player. Beyond the many records, Henderson is known for his discipline. He truly understood the value of properly executing the fundamentals well, and opposing teams sometimes shook their heads and watched as he did so with remarkable skill.

In 1979, his first year on the major leagues, Henderson had 33 steals in 89 games over four months. In 1980, however, he stole 100, breaking records that dated back to the turn of the century. He also batted .303 and led the American League by reaching base 301 times. This marked the start of a long record-breaking career.

Rickey Nelson Henley Henderson was born on Christmas Day, 1958, in the backseat of an Oldsmobile on the way to the hospital. As Henderson later joked, "I was always fast. I couldn't wait." His parents, John and Bobbie Henley, lived in Chicago. When he was seven years old—five years after his father had left—his mother packed up the family and moved them to Oakland, California. There, Bobbie met Paul Henderson, and they married while Rickey was in high school. Her five kids took the Henderson last name.

Henderson attended Oakland Technical High School, where he excelled in three sports: baseball, basketball, and football. Of the three sports, his first love was football, and he was an All-American running back. When he graduated from high school in 1976, Henderson could have pursued either a college scholarship to play football or a path toward professional baseball. His mother helped steer him toward a career in baseball, arguing that football players had shorter careers.

FAST FACTS

- During his first season with the New York Yankees, Henderson became the first major league player in history to enter the "80/20 club" (with 80 steals and 24 home runs), and he repeated the feat the next year, with 87 steals and 28 homers.

- Henderson led the American League with 66 steals in 1998 (with the Oakland A's), making him the oldest stolen base leader in major league history.

- His most impressive record of all, however, is for total stolen bases. At 1,406 bases stolen, Henderson's career record will likely stand for a very long time.

The Oakland Athletics drafted Henderson in 1976, and he began to work his way through the minor leagues. In his second year with the Modesto A's, he won the team's Most Valuable Player trophy for 95 steals. Henderson made his major league debut in June 1979.

Henderson saw early on that the secret to success was to become an expert at reading pitchers. He was taught that leadoff hitters have a specific role to play—work the pitch count in order to get on base to then advance and score. Though he would later break records for leadoff home runs, he was also a league leader in walks. But above all, his ability to read the pitcher and time pitches set him apart when it came to base stealing. These disciplines would define his career.

Although the 1981 season was shortened by a players' strike, Henderson led the American League in hits, runs, and steals. The next year was even more extraordinary. He stole 130 bases during the 1982 season, surpassing the total steals of nine of the American League's 14 teams. And he continued in 1983, when he posted his third year of breaking records for runs, stolen bases, and walks.

The New York Yankees acquired Henderson in December 1984. During his time in New York, Henderson set the franchise record for stolen bases (326). After a midseason trade back to Oakland in

1989, Henderson kept his momentum. His performance led the A's into the postseason and a World Series championship.

In 1990, Henderson's batting average fell below .320 for only one game, and he again led the league in runs and stolen bases. In fact, Henderson led the league in stolen bases every year from 1980 to 1991, with the exception of 1987. He also won the American League's MVP Award in 1990, leading the A's to another pennant. On May 1 the next year, Henderson finally broke the career stolen base record set by Lou Brock when he stole base number 939.

In 1993, Oakland traded Henderson to the Toronto Blue Jays, who were on their way to the postseason. From that 1993 season through the end of his career in 2003, Henderson was traded nine times and played for seven different teams. He continued to put up respectable numbers, but his career had turned a corner.

In 2001, at age 42, he broke three major records while with the San Diego Padres: career walks (2,179), career runs (2,288), and career games in left field. This marked the 23rd consecutive season in which he had 20 or more steals. On top of that, on the final day of the 2001 season, Henderson collected his 3,000th career hit.

Throughout his entire career, Henderson worked hard to stay in shape. During interviews, he described focusing on stretching and keeping flexible instead of lifting weights. This helped him keep his speed when running. He truly loved fulfilling his role of helping his team succeed. His disciplined approach to keeping fit was an important way for him to do this. After retiring reluctantly from playing, he coached other players, demonstrating that when it comes to pursuing your passion, where there's a will, there is always a way.

RUNNERS-UP

CARL YASTRZEMSKI

Carl Yastrzemski played his entire 23-year career with the Boston Red Sox. He is the team's record holder for RBIs, hits, runs scored, and games played, among other firsts. At the age of 80, he was still working with young athletes during spring training.

TIM RAINES

Tim Raines is definitely one of the best leadoff hitters in baseball history. He played most of his career with the Montreal Expos and earned four National League stolen base titles in the early 1980s. Despite being diagnosed with lupus, a condition in which patients' organs come under attack by their own body, he prevailed and returned to the field after receiving treatment.

Legendary Great

TED WILLIAMS

To say that Ted Williams is a legend is an understatement. This is especially true given that his career was put on hold twice for the five years he spent serving his country—first during World War II and later during the Korean War.

Here are just some of his career stats: a .344 batting average, 2,654 hits, 521 home runs, 1,839 RBIs, and an on-base percentage of .4817 (the best in baseball history). But the stat that people probably remember the most came in 1941, when Williams ended the season with a .406 batting average. On the last day of the season, Williams and the Red Sox were playing a double-header against the Philadelphia Athletics. Both teams were well out of contention for the postseason. Going into that Sunday, Williams's average stood at .3995, and the Red Sox manager offered to let him sit out the game. His season average would be .400 once it was rounded up. Williams declined. He then batted 6–8. That was the last time a player has topped .400 in a single season.

Spotlight

GREATEST TEAM

The Cincinnati Reds absolutely ruled the National League throughout the 1970s, and the team fielding at mid-decade is considered to be one of the best in MLB history. The team was so dominating that it earned the nickname "Big Red Machine." With the exception of the 1971 season, the Reds reached 90-plus wins every year. It won six NL West division titles and four NL pennants. And in 1976, it became the first NL team since the early 1920s to win back-to-back World Series titles.

The team reached its peak in 1975 and 1976 with a core lineup that earned its own nickname, the "Great Eight." Led by manager Sparky Anderson, the Great Eight's starting lineup included Johnny Bench, Pete Rose, Joe Morgan, Tony Pérez, Dave Concepción, George Foster, Ken Griffey Sr., and César Gerónimo. Between them, the Great Eight took home three batting titles, four home-run titles, six MVP Awards, 26 Gold Gloves, and a ridiculous 65 All-Star selections.

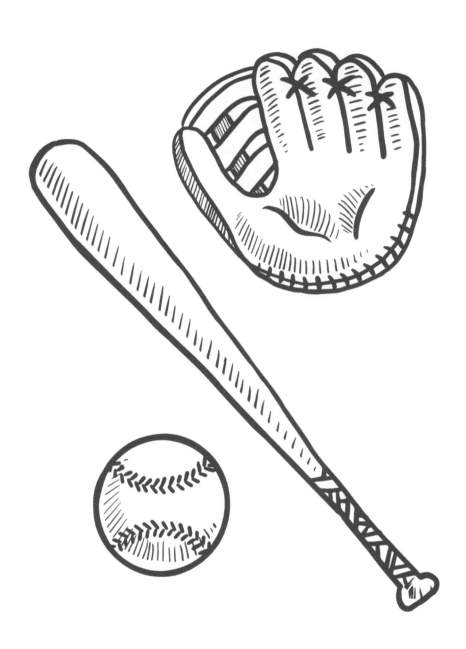

KEN GRIFFEY JR.

CENTER FIELD

90

KEN GRIFFEY JR.

HEIGHT: 6'3" | WEIGHT: 195LB
BORN: NOVEMBER 21, 1969
DONORA, PA

CAREER STATS

G	AB	R	H	2B	3B
2.671	9.801	1.662	2.781	524	38

HR	RBI	BB	AVG	OBP	SLG
630	1.836	1.312	.284	.370	.538

13X ALL-STAR
10X GOLD GLOVE
7X SILVER SLUGGER

*"As long as I have fun playing,
the stats will take care of themselves."*

1989-2010

Imagine not only making it to the major leagues but also getting to play with your father. Ken Griffey Jr.'s father was still playing ball (for the Reds) when Griffey's baseball career took off. In August 1990, father and son found themselves not only on the same lineup card but also batting side-by-side in the order. They were the first father and son ever to play at the same time in the major leagues. The Griffeys hit back-to-back singles to start off the game. Two weeks later, in September, the pair hit back-to-back home runs.

Griffey hit his 500th home run on Father's Day 2004 despite struggling with various injuries that year. Though that made him just the 20th major league player to reach that milestone, this was a truly important milestone because it was his dad, a fellow major leaguer, who first instilled a passion for the game in him.

George Kenneth Griffey Jr. was born on November 21, 1969, in Pennsylvania. His family moved to Cincinnati, Ohio, when he was six years old. His father, Ken Sr., played in the outfield for the Cincinnati Reds and was a member of the unbeatable "Big Red Machine" of the 1970s. During those years, it was common for Griffey to run around the Reds clubhouse, getting to know the players. Meanwhile, his father taught him to be a team player, stressing team accomplishments over individual ones. Reds players from that era remember that he was a confident, likeable kid.

Griffey attended Archbishop Moeller High School. In 1987, during his senior year, he was named the United States High School Baseball Player of the Year. A baseball future was clearly to come. Later that year, the Seattle Mariners selected Griffey as their number-one draft pick. Perhaps because he had spent so many years in Ohio, when he heard he was going to the Mariners, he walked into the house and jokingly said, "Hey, Dad, where's Seattle?"

Griffey entered the Mariners minor league system when he was just 17 years old. He batted .313, with 14 home runs during his first season and was considered the league's number-one prospect. However, his minor league career didn't last long. The pitching at that level was no match for him, and Griffey easily strode through to the majors. He joined the Seattle Mariners after just two years in the minor leagues.

Griffey's debut in the majors came on Opening Day in 1989. The Mariners were facing the Oakland A's, the defending American League champions, and Griffey hit a double in his first at bat as a rookie. The fans in Seattle couldn't wait to see more of the new kid, who clearly had a lot of talent. A week later, in his first at bat in his home stadium, he hit his first home run. Griffey continued to dominate for the Mariners, batting .300 and .327 during 1990 and 1991, respectively.

Throughout the 1990s, Griffey was exemplary in the outfield. He won the American League's Gold Glove Award every year of the decade. And in 1997, he was voted the American League's Most Valuable Player. Off the field, he became the new face of Seattle baseball. The fans readily embraced Griffey's loveable personality—the big smile and the hat turned backward—flocking to the games to see him play. Griffey showed the fans that he was truly enjoying himself.

In early 2000, on his own prompting, Griffey was acquired by the Cincinnati Reds. He yearned to be closer to his family. Plus, Griffey considered Cincinnati his hometown, and Ken Sr. was coaching there after retiring as a player. Once he made the move to the Reds, he started out with a typical Griffey year, hitting 40 home runs. From 2001 through 2004, however, Griffey averaged just 80 games per season. Constant injuries kept him off the field.

Griffey was traded to the Chicago White Sox in mid-2008, but played just 41 games for them that season. After much thought, he returned to the fans who were dearest to him, signing with the Seattle Mariners in early 2009. The Mariners enjoyed robust attendance that year as a result.

Griffey was raised in the bright lights of his father's career and was surrounded by attention until his retirement in 2010. He managed to always stay confident, which showed in his general positivity and infectious personality. As Edgar Martinez put it: "Junior obviously had all the tools and skills to play the game. The ability is one part. The other part is always being very confident in his ability. This game is a lot about confidence. You can have skills, but not be confident. Junior had that combination. That made him special." His confidence allowed him to be a good team player, as he would always try to focus on the needs and accomplishments of his team.

Off the field, Griffey has worked to help children who are less fortunate than he was as a child. The Ken Griffey Jr. Foundation supports several children's hospitals, as well as the Boys & Girls Clubs of America.

FAST FACTS

- Griffey is tied with Don Mattingly and Dale Long for the record of most (8) consecutive games with a home run.

- Griffey's .300 batting average and 22 home runs in 1990 earned him his first trip to the All-Star Game. He would be an All-Star 13 times throughout his career.

- Griffey hit his 600th homer in 2008, joining the ranks of a very select few. Only four other players at the time had hit more.

RUNNERS-UP

MICKEY MANTLE

Mickey Mantle is arguably the greatest switch-hitter in major league history, despite playing most of his career plagued by chronic leg injuries. He was a four-time home-run champion in the 1950s, and he appeared in seven World Series. In his later years, he turned to philanthropy, raising money for victims of the 1995 Oklahoma City bombing and to raise awareness of organ donation.

JOE DIMAGGIO

Joe DiMaggio played for just 13 years, but he appeared in the All-Star Game every year. He took home nine World Series rings during that time. Highly regarded as a powerful hitter, he is most known for his 56-game hitting streak, a record that will likely stand for a very long time. Although his father had hoped he would become a fisherman like him, DiMaggio had the courage to pursue his own dream of playing baseball.

Legendary Great

WILLIE MAYS

Coaches, managers, and baseball writers all like to talk about the tools a player has. "Player X is a five-tool player," they'll say. The five tools are speed, arm strength, fielding ability, hitting for average, and hitting for power. Regarded as possibly the greatest five-tool player, Willie Mays put up the numbers to prove it. Ted Williams, another baseball great, said, "They invented the All-Star Game for Willie Mays."

Mays ended his 22-year career with a .302 batting average, 3,283 hits, 660 home runs (the fifth most in all of baseball), and 1,903 RBIs. He is one of five National League players to have eight consecutive 100-RBI seasons. On the field, he earned 12 consecutive Gold Gloves, and his career fielding percentage only dipped below .970 once. Mays played for the Giants all but four of his years in professional baseball. Though the Giants retired his number in 1972, at the end of his tenure there, the Mets have not. But few players dare to wear it. Mays spent his last two seasons with the Mets.

Prior to that, he had a two-year stint in the US Army. Mays received a Presidential Medal of Freedom in 2015. During the ceremony, President

Barack Obama said, "Willie also served our country: In his quiet example while excelling on one of America's biggest stages, [he] helped carry forward the banner of civil rights. It's because of giants like Willie that someone like me could even think about running for president."

Players From Around the World

CUBA

Baseball was first introduced to Cuba during the 1860s. It's unclear who brought the first bats and balls—American sailors or Cuban students who had been studying in the US—or if the sport came to the island simply from its proximity to the US. Nonetheless, the first organized game played between Cuban teams took place in 1874.

The Cuban Winter League, the second oldest professional baseball league, formed in 1878 and gradually increased in local popularity throughout the next couple decades. Then, in the early 1900s, interest in the league took off after American players discovered that they could continue to play ball there year-round. Players from both the Negro Leagues and the majors quickly helped mature the quality of play in the Cuban League.

Conversely, Cuban-born players often migrated to the US leagues. Even though Jackie Robinson unquestionably broke the color barrier for black players in 1947, Latin American players made it into the big leagues decades earlier. In fact, more than 50 Latinx players had made it to the major leagues, and 230-plus made it to the Negro Leagues.

Meanwhile, the Cuban government of the early 1950s was overthrown, and a new leader, Fidel Castro, instituted communism, a form of governance in which all property is equally owned by everyone and people are paid for the work they do according to their needs. In 1961, Castro banned all professional sports in the country. The Cuban Winter League came to an end after a glorious run. Cuban baseball players were also forbidden from playing abroad, meaning their only route to the majors was by defecting, or abandoning their country.

Since the revolution, more than 80 players have defected and made it to the big leagues. Some well-known Cuban players who have made it to the majors include Yoennis Céspedes, Aroldis Chapman, Orlando "El Duque" Hernández, Yasiel Puig, and Luis Tiant. The list of minor leaguers who fled their country to play baseball is even greater (90).

ICHIRO SUZUKI

RIGHT FIELD

102

51

ICHIRO SUZUKI

HEIGHT: 5'11" | WEIGHT: 175LB
BORN: OCTOBER 22, 1973
NICHI KASUGAI-GUN, JAPAN

CAREER STATS

G	AB	R	H	2B	3B
2,653	9,934	1,420	3,089	362	96

HR	RBI	BB	AVG	OBP	SLG
117	780	647	.311	.355	.402

10X ALL-STAR
10X GOLD GLOVE
3X SILVER SLUGGER

"I've always prided myself in not reveling in past accomplishments and focusing on future achievement instead. That's been my career motto."

2001-2019

When Ichiro Suzuki made it to the big leagues, he knew that he was making a big move. He would be trying to excel at playing against teams and players that he knew almost nothing about. Moreover, he would be meeting players who were well known and highly regarded. Ichiro had many reasons to want to make a good impression. Instead of appearing overconfident, Ichiro set about showing his respect for the game.

Despite being on the smaller side, Ichiro worked hard to excel. It paid off. In 2016, Ichiro stole his 500th major league base in April. Four months later, in August, he collected his 3,000th MLB career hit with a triple.

Ichiro was born on October 22, 1973, in Japan, and grew up in a very small town named Toyoyama. He joined his first baseball team at age seven, and by age 12, he had dedicated himself to playing the game for life. He and his father had a rigorous daily practice routine, because Suzuki was determined to become the best player possible. The word "concentration" was inscribed on his glove as a reminder to remain focused.

Ichiro attended Aikodai Meiden High School, which had a prestigious baseball program. He trained hard during high school, throwing car tires and hitting balls with a shovel to build up his strength and endurance to make up for his smaller frame. He stood at five feet, nine inches and weighed just 124 pounds. Despite stellar performance in high school—he batted .505—he wasn't drafted into the Nippon Professional Baseball (NPB) league until the final round because of his size.

Ichiro made his professional debut in Japan in 1992, at 18 years of age, for a team called the Orix Blue Wave. From the beginning, Ichiro had an unorthodox swing that worried his managers. After batting .385 in 1994—a league record—the doubts ended. He also dropped his last name, Suzuki, from his jersey at the urging of his manager. Suzuki is a very common name in Japan, and the manager wanted Ichiro to stand out.

Following the 1996 season, and again in 1998, Ichiro played in a series of exhibition games against visiting teams made up of MLB All-Stars. Seeing the caliber of play by the Americans kindled Ichiro's interest in major league ball. Unfortunately, he was under contract for several more years.

When the Blue Wave fell out of contention in 2000, the team's owners reluctantly agreed to make Ichiro eligible for a move to the American leagues. The Seattle Mariners were so excited by Ichiro's potential that they immediately signed him. Ichiro was the first Japanese position player to move to the major leagues.

When Ichiro signed with the Mariners, he knew that he was making a very difficult move. "Sometimes I am nervous, sometimes anxious, but I want to challenge a new world," he said in a *Sports Illustrated* interview. A big part of that challenge was the language barrier, so Ichiro made sure that his baseball contract included English lessons for both him and his wife.

FAST FACTS

- In 2009, Ichiro reached his 2,000th major league hit.

- Ichiro won his sixth Gold Glove Award and appeared in his sixth All-Star Game in 2006. This was his sixth year in the majors.

Throughout his nine years in Japan's Nippon Professional Baseball, Ichiro batted .353 and won seven Golden Glove Awards. Still, many Americans questioned whether he could succeed at the major league level. Ichiro had yet to set foot onto an American field.

When Ichiro joined the Seattle Mariners, the team issued him the same jersey number that star pitcher

Randy Johnson had previously worn. Ichiro appreci-
ated this honor, and to show his respect, Ichiro wrote
to Johnson, saying that he would not bring shame
to the number. He proceeded to keep his promise
right from day one. Ichiro debuted with the Seattle
Mariners in 2001 and had a remarkable rookie
season, with 242 hits, a .350 batting average, and
56 stolen bases. He also won the American League's
Most Valuable Player Award and the Rookie of the
Year Award.

Ichiro continued his success in 2002, batting .321,
with 208 hits. In 2004, he finished the season with
262 hits, breaking the single-season records for both
MLB and NPB. During the next four seasons, Ichiro
continued to post outstanding numbers. In 2010, he
finished the season with 214 hits, making it the 10th
straight 200-plus hit season. (Ichiro had 210 hits for
the Orix Blue Wave in 1994, so this was actually his
11th season above the 200 mark.)

Ichiro's performance fell off in 2012, and fearing
he might be hurting the team, he asked to be traded.
Ichiro had tremendous respect for his teammates.
The New York Yankees took him in, moving him
to left field (he was normally a right fielder) and
the bottom of the batting order—two moves that
reflected his decreased production. Ichiro remained
a threat, however, batting .322 that year. The Miami
Marlins picked up Ichiro at the end of 2014. They

originally planned for him to be a backup outfielder, but he ended up appearing in 64 of the first 68 games.

In the spring of 2018, Ichiro re-signed with the Seattle Mariners. In his way, he accepted because he wanted to thank the team, as well as the fans, for the opportunity to play in the major leagues. The team added him to the active roster for the 2019 season opener to be played against the Oakland A's in the Tokyo Dome in Japan. Ichiro was finally able to play a professional game before an adoring crowd in his home country. At the end of game 2 he announced his retirement, even though he was only 15 games into the season.

Over the years, Ichiro never lost sight of the difficulties that foreign players faced. He learned enough English to have casual conversations with those around him, and he even learned some Spanish phrases and taught his teammates a little Japanese. It was important to him that he showed respect for both the history of the game and everyone he came into contact with. At the same time, he remembered his roots, donating $1.25 million to the Japanese Red Cross in 2011 for earthquake and tsunami relief.

He also hopes the work ethic that got him to the major leagues serves as an inspiration for others. He once said, "I'm not a big guy, and hopefully kids could look at me and see that I'm not muscular and not physically imposing, that I'm just a regular guy. So if somebody with a regular body can get into the record books, kids can look at that. That would make me happy." Ichiro chairs the Ichiro Cup, a boys' league tournament held in Japan over a six-month period.

RUNNERS-UP

TONY GWYNN

Tony Gwynn, nicknamed "Mr. Padre," won eight batting titles in his 20-year career playing for the San Diego Padres. He holds the record of the highest career batting average of any Padres player, and he batted above .300 for every year after his rookie season. He was known for his strong work ethic. He would not only participate in extra batting practice whenever possible but also study video recordings of his games carefully to see where he could improve.

REGGIE JACKSON

Reggie Jackson earned the nickname "Mr. October" because of his uncanny ability to outperform in the postseason. In five trips to the World Series, he batted .357 and hit 10 home runs. At the end of his 21-year career, he had 563 home runs, putting him at 14th on the list of leaders. Despite sustaining injuries during his youth that doctors said would prevent him from walking and playing sports again, he worked hard to overcome his physical limitations and went on to have a remarkable career.

ROBERTO CLEMENTE

Roberto Clemente was the first Latin American to star in Major League Baseball and a hero to all Puerto Rican players to follow. Known for a powerful throwing arm from the outfield, he also won National League batting titles four times. He was the first Latin American to be inducted into the Baseball Hall of Fame. During the off-seasons, he spent time delivering food and baseball equipment to those in need across Latin America and the Caribbean. He was on his way to deliver aid to victims of an earthquake in Nicaragua when his plane went down in 1972.

Legendary Great

HANK AARON

For more than three decades, Hank Aaron was known as the home-run king. And many today still regard him as the true home-run leader, as well as possibly the best power hitter in baseball history. Former teammate Joe Adock once said, "Trying to sneak a fastball past Hank Aaron is like trying to sneak the sunrise past a rooster."

Nicknamed "Hammerin' Hank," Aaron passed Babe Ruth's home-run record of 714 in 1974 and went on to finish his career with a record 755. He held this record until Barry Bonds surpassed it in 2007. He also holds a career batting average of .305 and records for the most RBIs, extra-base hits, and total bases. He was the first player to reach both 3,000 hits and 500 home runs. In addition, Aaron won three Gold Gloves for his fielding and was named the National League's MVP in 1957.

Aaron ended his career not on the field, but as a baseball executive, making him one of the first minorities in the major leagues to reach upper management. He became a businessman and prominent community figure. In 2001, he received the Presidential Citizens Medal, and in 2002, he was awarded the Presidential Medal of Freedom.

Beating the Odds

CURTIS PRIDE

Originally signed by the New York Mets, Curtis Pride reached the major leagues in 1993 with the Montreal Expos. When he joined the team, Pride became the first deaf player in more than 45 years to reach the majors. Born deaf as a consequence of rubella (German measles), Pride became a fluent lip reader early in life.

Throughout his 11-year career in the majors, Pride played for six different teams. Though he did not play regularly—he either pinch hit or played the field as an injury replacement—he was an excellent fielder with a strong arm. In 1996, Pride received the Tony Conigliaro Award for overcoming adversity. Following his career in the majors, Pride became the baseball coach at Gallaudet University in Washington, DC, a private school for individuals who are deaf and hard of hearing.

EDGAR MARTINEZ

DESIGNATED HITTER

114

EDGAR MARTINEZ

HEIGHT: 6'0" | WEIGHT: 175LB
BORN: JANUARY 2, 1963
NEW YORK, NY

CAREER STATS

G	AB	R	H	2B	3B
2,055	7,213	1,219	2,247	514	15

HR	RBI	BB	AVG	OBP	SLG
309	1,261	1,283	.312	.418	.515

7X ALL-STAR
5X SILVER SLUGGER
2X BATTING TITLE

*"We don't mention anything that is negative.
We focus on what we want to accomplish."*

1987-2004

While growing up in Puerto Rico, Edgar Martinez looked up to baseball hero Roberto Clemente, a fellow Puerto Rican. Clemente was celebrated for both his exceptional play on the field and his local charity work. It was Clemente's performance in the 1971 World Series that inspired Martinez to learn the game.

Martinez did not stand out as a star when he first joined the pros. But as someone who understood the value of hard work, he was dedicated to self-improvement, practicing hard, changing his diet, and meditating. His breakout year at the plate came in 1995. He batted .356 and led the American League in runs scored, doubles, and on-base percentage. These numbers won him a second Silver Slugger Award. Moreover, his performance helped lead the Mariners to their first Division Series title. That season, Martinez also won his first Outstanding Designated Hitter Award.

Edgar Martinez was born on January 2, 1963, in New York City to José and Christina Salgado Martinez. His parents divorced when he was two years old, and he went to live with his grandparents in Puerto Rico. Several years later, his parents renewed their marriage, but Martinez chose to remain with his grandparents instead of returning to the United States.

By the time Martinez was 19, he was playing in a semiprofessional league in Puerto Rico. He was not a flashy player—in fact, he was an introvert. But he hit well, possibly better than most. Upon finishing high school, he enrolled in the Interamerican University of Puerto Rico, where he studied business administration. He also had two jobs, working in a furniture store during the day and in a factory at night. Despite that, he found time to play semi-professional baseball.

When his coach encouraged him to attend a tryout sponsored by the Seattle Mariners, Martinez caught the eye of a scout, who thought Martinez might have promise. The Mariners signed him to a contract in 1982. The move to the Mariners team was a big adjustment, and Martinez got off to a slow start. As he described it, he knew he could hit, but something was holding him back. He finally realized that if he changed his habits—including his mind-set—he could achieve success.

Martinez spent seven seasons in the minor leagues, where he worked hard to perfect his skills. He focused on individual hitting drills, such as hitting off of a tee, to the point of exhaustion. He meditated to keep his mind focused, and he developed a nutrition plan that he would stick with for his entire career. All his hard work had the effect of strengthening his abilities, which built his confidence. By 1987, his potential was finally recognized.

From 1987 through 1989, Martinez spent short stints with the big-league team. Though he was named the starting third baseman for the Mariners at the beginning of the 1989 season, he was sent back to the minor leagues briefly. Martinez was added full-time to the Mariners roster in 1990. He was promoted to starting third baseman a couple weeks into the 1990 season.

The Mariners had several big-name players on the team in those days (Randy Johnson and Ken Griffey Jr., among others), and Martinez was content to stay in the background. He didn't need the fanfare to confirm that he was good. His hard work and results told him that. But in 1992, Martinez broke out with a .343 batting average and 181 hits in 135 games. The next two seasons, 1993 and 1994, were both shortened by injury, and he began to see time as the designated hitter. By 1995, he was a full-time designated hitter.

Although he was used primarily as the DH at this point, Martinez played one game at third base in 1996. He batted .327 that season with 163 hits over 139 games. His 1,000th career hit came in late August. Martinez won his second and third Outstanding Designated Hitter Awards in 1997 and 1998, respectively. His performance helped the team reach the postseason yet again.

A nagging hamstring and other injuries plagued Martinez in 2002 and 2003. He hit his 2,000th hit in 2003 and played well enough to be named to the All-Star team. But a foot injury in September ended his season early. The 2004 season brought yet more injuries, and the team started experimenting with a new designated hitter. In early August, it was clear to Martinez that the time to retire had come.

FAST FACTS

- At the end of his first full season in the majors, Martinez had a batting average of .302, and he led the team in on-base percentage. In 1991, his second full season in the majors, he hit a career high of .307.

- Martinez's performance in 1992 earned him his first Silver Slugger Award and brought the Mariners their first franchise batting title.

- Martinez's tenth season posting a .300-plus average was in 2001. He won both the Silver Slugger Award and the Outstanding Designated Hitter Award that year.

Throughout his 18-year career, Martinez made seven All-Star Game appearances and won five Silver Slugger Awards. Moreover, he won the Outstanding Designated Hitter Award five times. He was the quiet leader in the back of the room, beloved by his teammates and by the fans because he had learned to never let doubt creep in. Martinez's career was defined by perseverance. He knew that if he just kept going, he could achieve his goals.

Following his retirement, he donated time and money to the Seattle Children's Hospital. The Mariners established the Edgar Martinez Endowment for Muscular Dystrophy Research in his honor, as well as the Children's Hospital Annual Wishing Well Night. Martinez also became involved with other children's charities, including Make-A-Wish, Big Brothers Big Sisters of America, United Way, and Page Ahead Children's Literacy Program. His charity work earned him a spot in the World Sports Humanitarian Hall of Fame.

RUNNERS-UP

PAUL MOLITOR

Paul Molitor was one of the first players to enter the Hall of Fame with DH credentials. With 3,319 hits, a .306 career average, and 504 stolen bases, Molitor is just one of four players to achieve those milestones. None of the others played the game after 1930. Molitor overcame various major injuries early in his career to continue playing the sport he so loved.

CHARLES "CHILI" DAVIS

Charles "Chili" Davis is the first Jamaican-born player to make it to the major leagues. He became almost exclusively a designated hitter when he switched to the American League in the second half of his 19 years as a player. He hit 350 home runs during his career and is distinguished for hitting a home run from each side of the plate in a single game nine times. He got the nickname "Chili" when as a child, his father gave him a bad haircut, and the neighborhood children joked that it looked like someone had placed a chili bowl on his head. A good sense of humor led him to keep the nickname into adulthood.

Spotlight

THE DESIGNATED HITTER RULE

Even if it may seem as though the designated hitter has been a part of baseball forever, it is a relatively new addition. As early as 1906, the idea of a designated hitter rose up in conversations among players, managers, and owners. Pitchers were notoriously poor batters, and adding a tenth player who would permanently pinch hit in the pitcher's spot might add an offensive jolt that would draw more fans. Still, the idea teetered off until the 1960s, when dominant pitchers like Bob Gibson (1.12 ERA) all but shut down scoring. More scoring means more exciting games.

In the early 1970s, Charlie Finley, then-owner of the Oakland A's, revitalized the idea of the designated hitter, hoping to boost attendance. On January 11, 1973, baseball owners voted to institute the designated hitter in the American League in a three-year experiment. The National League resisted. The results in the American League were immediate, both in terms of higher batting averages and larger crowds, and the designated hitter became a permanent fixture in the AL. However, use of the designated hitter (Official Baseball Rule 5.11) is actually optional. Though rare, several teams have occasionally opted not to use the designated hitter, arguably giving the manager greater flexibility.

Beating the Odds

BO JACKSON

In the history of professional sports, it's unheard-of for someone to play for both a professional football team and a Major League Baseball team at the same time. Vincent Edward "Bo" Jackson did just that. After graduating from Auburn University in 1986, Jackson was drafted by the Kansas City Royals, and he debuted in the majors that September. Meanwhile, Jackson was also chosen in the 1986 NFL Draft by the Tampa Bay Buccaneers, but he chose not to play for them. The next year, Jackson was again chosen in the NFL Draft, this time by the Los Angeles Raiders, who agreed to allow him to play the entire baseball season before joining the team.

Jackson racked up impressive stats for both teams, and soon became a media star as well, thanks to a popular Nike shoe campaign. But Jackson's football career came to a sudden end in 1990 when a tackle by a Cincinnati Bengals player dislocated his hip. Ultimately, he needed a hip replacement.

Many thought his return to the majors was unrealistic. Not one to accept limits, Jackson joined the Chicago White Sox in 1993, where he went on to hit 16 home runs and drive in 45 RBIs. He also returned to school to complete his degree, dabbled in television and video games, invested in a community bank, served as the HealthSouth Sports Medicine Council's president, and helped raise more than $1 million for emergency disaster relief.

Honorable Mention

FRANK THOMAS

Frank Thomas was born and raised in Columbus, Georgia. He excelled in both baseball and football during high school. Though he dreamed of playing professional baseball, no team drafted him when he graduated. So, he went to Auburn University to play football.

People said he wouldn't be a baseball player, but Thomas didn't listen. He went on to be one of the best hitters in baseball history. Thomas is the only player ever to hit 20 or more home runs and average .300 or better in seven consecutive seasons. He was a five-time All-Star and was named the American League's Most Valuable Player an incredible two years in a row. Nicknamed "The Big Hurt" for the way he crushed home runs, Thomas spent most of his career with the Chicago White Sox. He credits his belief in himself to his early involvement in the local Boys & Girls Club of Columbus. Today, he gives back generously to the clubs in Chicago.

TONY LA RUSSA

MANAGER

126

10

TONY LA RUSSA

HEIGHT: 6'0" | WEIGHT: 175LB
BORN: OCTOBER 4, 1944
TAMPA, FL

MANAGERIAL RECORD
WINS: 2,728

CHICAGO WHITE SOX
1979-1986

OAKLAND ATHLETICS
1986-1995

3 PENNANTS AND 1 WORLD SERIES TITLE

ST. LOUIS CARDINALS
1996-2011

3 PENNANTS AND 2 WORLD SERIES TITLES

1979-2011

Tony La Russa was a true pioneer when it came to managing baseball teams. When he entered the league, he observed that everyone played the game a certain way and that no one questioned why. So, he started to experiment. He asked, "How might we keep a player fresh and interested over the long season? Are there any unique ways to score runs?" Being willing to ask such questions led to a noteworthy career.

Anthony La Russa Jr. was born in 1944 in Tampa, Florida. His parents, Anthony and Olivia, met while they were both working at a cigar factory. His father's family came from Sicily and his mother's came from Spain. La Russa grew up speaking Spanish. Baseball was a big part of the community where La Russa was raised, and he naturally took to the game early.

He played well enough in Jefferson High School in Tampa that several major league teams noticed him. Upon graduation, he was signed by the Kansas City Athletics as a middle infielder while also attending college. He earned a degree in industrial management from the University of South Florida and then went on to earn a law degree from Florida State University.

La Russa played for just six years in the majors. A shoulder injury in his first year limited his playing time, and he never fully realized his potential because of it. In those six years, he played for six different teams. Despite earning his law degree, baseball remained La Russa's passion.

In 1978, the Chicago White Sox offered him a job managing in their minor league system. The next year, he was tapped to be the manager of the big-league White Sox, because the team's owner had been impressed by La Russa's leadership abilities. In 1979, La Russa became the youngest manager in the major leagues. He immediately sought the advice of more experienced managers around the league.

It took La Russa two years to get his footing leading the team. But in his second year, he won the American League's Manager of the Year Award after he took the White Sox to the play-offs. Though he had some good years following that 1983 season, the team dismissed him in a front office shake-up in 1986. Many years later, the team's owner admitted that he regretted the move.

La Russa was not unemployed for long, though. Within three weeks, the Oakland A's hired him to manage their team. The team was in last place when he arrived in 1986, but finished the season well under his leadership. Over the next four years, La Russa quickly brought the team into winning form. He guided them to three World Series appearances from 1988 to 1990.

FAST FACTS

- ⚾ La Russa won his second Manager of the Year Award in 1988 and his third one in 1992.

- ⚾ Under La Russa's leadership, the Cardinals made it to the World Series in 2004 and 2006 and then again in 2011.

- ⚾ In his 16 years with Saint Louis, La Russa won more games than any other Cardinals manager.

La Russa brought a new managerial style to the game. He liked to experiment with the tried-and-true approaches, and he spent long hours studying both his own team and his opponents. He learned early on, for example, that over the course of a season, players become tired and a little lax. The question, then, was how to maintain his team's enthusiasm. He insisted that all base runners take leads off the bases, as if they were going to try to steal a base, even when the runners had no intention to steal. This kept them sharp by forcing them to pay attention so they didn't make an out by being picked off. The opposing team also had to pay attention in case the runner actually tried to steal. People remarked that even when the A's didn't win, they were certainly entertaining to watch.

After the 1995 season, however, the A's were sold to a new owner, and La Russa took a job with the Saint Louis Cardinals. The Cardinals were coming off several years of poor performance and needed a fresh start. In his first year there, La Russa brought the team to the playoffs. The Cardinals would remain strong throughout the 2000s. La Russa won his fourth Manager of the Year Award in 2002, this time in the National League. After a World Series win in 2011—the Cardinals also won the trophy in 2006—La Russa announced his retirement.

Over the course of his entire managing career, La Russa won 2,728 games, the third most of any major league manager (behind Connie Mack and John McGraw). He became known for his craftiness. In his time with the A's, for instance, La Russa started using a specialist pitcher called "the closer." The closing pitcher would be fresh off the bench, facing batters who were tired. The results spoke for themselves. Moreover, he then started swapping in other late-inning pitchers—inning by inning. They, too, would be fresh, able to maintain the lead left by the starter. Other teams took notice, and today these "specialist" pitchers are used by everyone.

Following his retirement, La Russa and his second wife founded Tony La Russa's Animal Rescue Foundation. He also ran programs to pair people in hospitals and abused children with homeless pets.

RUNNERS UP

JOHN MCGRAW

John McGraw managed for 33 years and recorded 2,763 wins. That's the second-most wins in baseball history. He was known and respected for seeing the potential in others and would often take chances on players that other teams turned down.

JOE TORRE

Joe Torre is the only major leaguer to record more than 2,000 hits as a player and 2,000 wins as a manager. His managing career lasted 29 seasons, and he guided the New York Yankees to four World Series championship trophies. Torre led an expedition to Cuba with other MLB officials and players in 2015 with the goal of improving relations between the two countries. The Torre Safe at Home Foundation works to prevent and address domestic violence.

SPARKY ANDERSON

Sparky Anderson is credited with driving the Cincinnati Reds to greatness in the mid-1970s, winning the World Series twice. Later, in the 1980s, he was named the American League's Manager of the Year in 1984 and 1987. He founded a charity dubbed CATCH—Caring Athletes Teamed for Children's and Henry Ford Hospitals—which helps seriously ill children without health insurance pay for their medical care.

Legendary Great

CONNIE MACK

Cornelius McGillicuddy, better known as Connie Mack, was born in 1862, six months before the Battle of Gettysburg. He decided at the age of 21 to make baseball his career, and he became the catcher of his local team. He is renowned for being one of the first players to use chatter to distract the batter. Years later, Mack became the player manager of the Pittsburgh Pirates.

Unlike the other managers of the day, he believed that he could get better results by treating players with respect instead of scolding them. Furthering the point, when he gave up playing, he wore a suit and tie (and a bowler hat) in the dugout. After a relatively short playing career—11 years—Mack took over as the manager of the Philadelphia Athletics and managed the team's first 50 seasons. Yes, that's 50 years. A true gentleman, Mack valued intelligence and good behavior in his players over raw ability alone. His philosophy worked. He holds the record for the most wins ever (3,731). He has nearly 1,000 wins more than any other manager and is the longest-serving manager in all of baseball history.

Spotlight

THE LONGEST GAME IN BASEBALL HISTORY

The longest game by innings occurred in May 1920, between the then-Boston Braves and the Brooklyn Robins (which later became the Dodgers). The game lasted 26 innings and ended in a tie when nightfall made playing impossible. Pitching changes were unheard of in 1920, so both starting pitchers played the whole game. Maybe the teams needed a bullpen.

Fast-forward to May 1984 and a game between the Milwaukee Brewers and the Chicago White Sox. This game lasted just 25 innings, but took two days to play. Total game time was eight hours, six minutes. (Side note: Carlton Fisk caught all 25 innings for the White Sox. Maybe they needed a backup catcher.)

However, the real winner here is the AAA game between the Rochester Red Wings and the Pawtucket Red Sox, played in 1981 at McCoy Stadium in Pawtucket, Rhode Island. This matchup lasted 33 innings, played over eight hours and 25 minutes. The first 32 innings were played on April 18 and 19, and the game was suspended on Sunday morning at 4:07 a.m., when the league president demanded that the teams stop playing. There were 19 fans left in the stands, each of whom received season or lifetime passes. The final 33rd inning was played on June 23, when the Red Wings were next in town. Pawtucket won the game, 3–2.

Create your own

STARTING LINEUP

	C
	1B
	2B
	3B
	SS
	LF
	CF
	RF
	DH

	LP
	RP

REFERENCES

Adomites, Paul, and Wisnia, Saul. "Babe Ruth." *How Stuff Works.* July 27, 2007. https://entertainment.howstuffworks.com/babe-ruth2.htm.

Armour, Mark. "Johnny Bench." *Society for American Baseball Research.* Last updated May 1, 2014. https://sabr.org/bioproj/person/aab28214.

Augustyn, Adam. "Bo Jackson." *Encyclopaedia Britannica.* Last updated September 20, 2019. https://www.britannica.com/biography/Bo-Jackson.

Author unknown. "Awards Named after Retired Closers." *ESPN.* https://www.espn.com/mlb/story/_/id/10756425/mariano-rivera-trevor-hoffman-new-awards-named-them.

Baldassaro, Lawrence. "Tony La Russa." *Society for American Baseball Research.* April 17, 2014. https://sabr.org/bioproj/person/6dbc8b54.

Baseball Almanac. "Eddie Mathews quotes." Accessed December 19, 2019. https://www.baseball-almanac.com/quotes/quomths.shtml.

Baseball Hall of Fame. "Eddie Mathews." Accessed December 19, 2019. https://baseballhall.org/hall-of-famers/mathews-eddie.

Baseball Historian. "Cuba Béisbol." http://www.baseballhistorian.com/cuba_baseball.cfm.

Baseball Reference. "History of Baseball in the Dominican Republic." Last updated March 7, 2019. https://www.baseball-reference.com/bullpen/History_of_baseball_in_the_Dominican_Republic.

Baseball Reference. "Tony LaRussa." Last updated November 2, 2017. https://www.baseball-reference.com/bullpen/Tony_LaRussa.

Belsky, Marta. "Living Loud: Curtis Pride—Major League Baseball Player." *Signing Savvy.* April 13, 2015. https://www.signingsavvy.com/blog/174/Living+Loud%3A+Curtis+Pride+Major+League+Baseball+Player.

Biography Archive. "Biography of Pedro Martinez." December 18, 2011. https://www.biographyarchive.com/biography-of-pedro-martinez.html.

Biography.com. "Joe DiMaggio." April 27, 2017; updated November 21, 2019. Accessed December 1, 2019. https://www.biography.com/athlete/joe-dimaggio.

Biography.com. "Lou Gehrig." April 27, 2017; updated April 15, 2019. Accessed December 1, 2019. https://www.biography.com/athlete/lou-gehrig.

Biography.com. "Willie Mays." November 23, 2015; updated September 30, 2019. Accessed December 1, 2019.https://www.biography.com/athlete /willie-mays.

Bush, Frederick C. "Craig Biggio." *Society for American Baseball Research*. Last updated July 8, 2015. https://sabr.org/bioproj/person /f4d29cc8.

Carroll, Will, and Nate Silver. "Prospectus Q&A: Rickey Henderson." *Baseball Prospectus*. January 12, 2009. https://www.baseballprospectus .com/news/article/2243/prospectus-qa-rickey-henderson/.

Celebrity Speakers Bureau. "Joe Torre." Accessed December 1, 2019. https://www.celebrityspeakersbureau.com/talent/joe-torre/.

Cortes, Ryan. "There's Never Been Anyone Quite Like Ken Griffey Jr." *The Undefeated*. July 25, 2016. https://theundefeated.com/features /theres-never-been-anyone-quite-like-ken-griffey-jr/.

Costello, Rory. "Chili Davis." *Society for American Baseball Research*. Last updated February 12, 2019. https://sabr.org/bioproj/person/f842dfbd.

The Daily Dose. "Johnny Bench: The greatest catcher in baseball history turns 68 years old today." December 7, 2015. http://dailydsports.com /johnny-bench/.

Dallas Morning News Editorial. "Texan of the Year Finalist Adrian Beltre Brought a Love of Baseball to Texas Rangers Fans." *The Dallas Morning News*. December 23, 2018. https://www.dallasnews.com/opinion /editorials/2018/12/23/texan-of-the-year-finalist-adrian-beltre-brought -a-love-of-baseball-to-texas-rangers-fans/.

Doyle, Jack. "Pitcher Perfect, 1963–1966." *The Pop History Dig*. Last updated June 17, 2019. https://www.pophistorydig.com/topics/tag /sandy-koufax-president-obama/.

Drayer, Shannon. "Edgar Martinez Is a Hall of Famer Because He Was Ahead of the Curve." *710 AM ESPN Seattle*. July 17, 2019. http://sports .mynorthwest.com/673622/drayer-edgar-martinez-ahead-of-curve/.

Encyclopaedia Britannica. "Nolan Ryan." Accessed October 1, 2019. https://www.britannica.com/biography/Nolan-Ryan.

Encyclopedia.com. "Connie Mack." Last updated September 27, 2019. https://www.encyclopedia.com/people/sports-and-games/sports -biographies/connie-mack.

Encyclopedia of World Biography. "Cal Ripken, Jr. Biography." Accessed December 1, 2019." https://www.notablebiographies.com/Pu-Ro/Ripken-Jr -Cal.html.

REFERENCES

Encyclopedia of World Biography. "Ichiro Suzuki Biography." Accessed October 1, 2019. https://www.notablebiographies.com/news/Sh-Z/Suzuki -Ichiro.html.

ESPN.com. "Bagwell Named Astros hitting coach." July 11, 2010. https:// www.espn.com/mlb/news/story?id=5371154.

ESPN.com. "Joe Torre, Sandy Koufax chat." February 27, 2018. https://www.espn.com/mlb/news/story?id=4953483.

ESPN.com. "Ted Williams." http://www.espn.com/mlb/player/bio /_/id/28096/ted-williams.

Faber, Charles F. "Joe Morgan." *Society for American Baseball Research.* Last updated May 1, 2014. https://sabr.org/bioproj/person/bf4f7a6e.

Faber, Charles F. "Ozzie Smith." *Society for American Baseball Research.* Last updated January 10, 2016. https://sabr.org/bioproj/person/a6663664.

The Famous People. "Ernie Banks Biography." Last updated September 16, 2016. https://www.thefamouspeople.com/profiles /ernie-banks-4274.php.

Feinstein, John. *Living on the Black.* New York: Little, Brown and Company, 2008.

Francis, Bill. "For Griffeys, Father's Day Is Always Special." *National Baseball Hall of Fame.* Accessed December 1, 2019. https://baseballhall .org/discover/for-griffeys-fathers-day-is-always-special.

Garro, Adrian. "Yasiel Puig Sometimes Thinks about Vanilla Ice Cream When Licking His Bat in the Batter's Box." *MLB.com's Cut4.* May 16, 2019. https://www.mlb.com/cut4/yasiel-puig-on-the-art-of-licking-baseball-bats.

Geller, Megan. "Ichiro Finishes a Magnificent MLB Career in Japan." *The Justice.* March 26, 2019. https://www.thejustice.org/article/2019/03 /ichiro-finishes-a-magnificent-mlb-career-in-japan.

Graney, Ed. "Peers Explain What Made Maddux Smartest Pitcher Ever." *Las Vegas Review-Journal,* July 27, 2014. https://www.reviewjournal.com /sports/sports-columns/ed-graney/peers-explain-what-made-maddux -smartest-pitcher-ever/.

Hample, Zack. *Watching Baseball Smarter.* New York: Vintage Books, 2007.

Harner, Andrew. "Jackie Robinson's Struggle as the First Black Player in MLB." *How They Play.* July 8, 2019. https://howtheyplay.com/team -sports/Jackie-Robinson-and-the-struggle-of-becoming-the-first-black -player-in-Major-League-Baseball.

REFERENCES

Harris, Scott, and Brian Boone. "The True Story Behind David Ortiz." Grunge. Accessed October 1, 2109. https://www.grunge.com/11890/true -story-behind-david-ortiz/.

Hummer, Steve. "For Chipper Jones, a Single-City Career and a Singular Atlanta Legacy." *Atlanta Journal-Constitution.* July 28, 2008. https:// www.ajc.com/sports/for-chipper-jones-single-city-career-and-singular -atlanta-legacy/HxSQBoM9Qlid5wewku2lRJ/.

Inspire21. "The Jim Abbott Story." http://inspire21.com/stories /sportsstories/TheJimAbbottStory.

Imaginesports.com. "The Life and Career of Hank Aaron." Diamond Mind Online. https://imaginesports.com/news/the-life-and-career-of -hank-aaron.

Infoplease. "The Longest Professional Baseball Game." Infoplease. https://www.infoplease.com/askeds/longest-professional-baseball-game.

Jockbio.com. "Andy Pettitte Biography." 2007. https://www.jockbio.com /Bios/Pettitte/Pettitte_bio.html.

King, Norm. "Tim Raines" *Society for American Baseball Research.* Last updated January 18, 2017. https://sabr.org/bioproj/person/6fb1015c.

Koichi. "A History of Japanese Baseball." Tofugu. March 26, 2013. https:// www.tofugu.com/japan/japanese-baseball-history/.

Koppett, Leonard. *Koppett's Concise History of Major League Baseball.* Philadelphia: Temple University Press, 1998.

Kroichick, Ron. "Randy Johnson in High School: 90 mph, Attitude." *SFGate.* June 1, 2009. https://www.sfgate.com/giants/article/Randy -Johnson-in-high-school-90-mph-attitude-3296537.php.

La Russa, Tony. *One Last Strike: Fifty Years in Baseball, Ten and a Half Games Back, and One Final Championship Season.* New York: William Morrow Paperbacks, 2013.

Laymance, Reid. "A Ray of Sunshine: Craig Biggio's Charity Work." *Houston Chronicle.* July 23, 2015. https://www.houstonchronicle.com /sports/astros/article/A-ray-of-sunshine-Craig-Biggio-s-charity-work -6401579.php.

Leggett, William. "Tom Seaver: 1969 Sportsman of the Year." *Sports Illustrated.* December 22, 1969. https://www.si.com/vault/1969/12/22 /618802/sportsman-of-the-year.

Look to the Stars. "David Ortiz Charity Work, Events, and Causes." Accessed December 1, 2019. https://www.looktothestars.org/celebrity /david-ortiz.

REFERENCES

Lougehrig.com. "Biography." Accessed October 1, 2019. https://www.lougehrig.com/biography/.

Mangin, Brad. "Greg Maddux." *National Baseball Hall of Fame.* Accessed December 1, 2019. https://baseballhall.org/hall-of-famers/maddux-greg.

McTaggart, Brian. "Biggio's Sunshine Kids Pin Approved by MLB." *Houston Chronicle.* March 30, 2007. https://www.chron.com/sports/astros/article/Biggio-s-Sunshine-Kids-pin-approved-by-MLB-1832914.php.

Miller, Bryce. "The Kid Provides the Show: Griffey Jr. wows in San Diego." *Associated Press,* July 8, 2016. https://www.apnews.com/ed9a33465c27451e8557aa38641ea6fd.

Miller, Kerry. "Major League Baseball's Top 10 Starting Pitchers of All Time." *Bleacher Report,* April 23, 2018. https://bleacherreport.com/articles/2770996-major-league-baseballs-top-10-starting-pitchers-of-all-time#slide0.

Mink, Michael. "Tony Gwynn Was a Major Hit Due to His Work Ethic." *Investor's Business Daily.* August 25, 2015. https://www.investors.com/news/management/leaders-and-success/tony-gwynn-was-a-hit-due-to-work-ethic/.

MLB.com. "Hoffman Achieved Athletic Goals with 1 Kidney," December 18, 2017. https://www.mlb.com/news/trevor-hoffman-overcomes-loss-of-kidney-c263735120.

Morgan, Chris. "Remembering Ichiro as a Hit Machine and as a Quote Machine." *Yahoo News,* June 15, 2016. https://www.yahoo.com/news/remembering-ichiro-hit-machine-quote-001207581.html.

National Baseball Hall of Fame. "Edgar Martinez." Accessed December 1, 2019. https://baseballhall.org/hall-of-famers/martinez-edgar.

National Baseball Hall of Fame. "Frank Thomas." Accessed December 1, 2019. https://baseballhall.org/hall-of-famers/thomas-frank.

National Baseball Hall of Fame. "Greg Maddux." Accessed December 1, 2019. https://baseballhall.org/hall-of-famers/maddux-greg.

National Baseball Hall of Fame. "Iván Rodríguez." Accessed December 1, 2019. https://baseballhall.org/hall-of-famers/rodriguez-ivan.

National Baseball Hall of Fame. "Paul Molitor." Accessed December 1, 2019. https://baseballhall.org/hall-of-famers/molitor-paul.

National Baseball Hall of Fame. "Roberto Alomar." Accessed December 1, 2019. https://baseballhall.org/hall-of-famers/alomar-roberto.

REFERENCES

National Baseball Hall of Fame. "Roberto Clemente." Accessed December 1, 2019. https://baseballhall.org/hall-of-famers/clemente-roberto.

National Baseball Hall of Fame. "Tom Seaver." Accessed December 1, 2019. https://baseballhall.org/hall-of-famers/seaver-tom.

National Baseball Hall of Fame. "Trevor Hoffman." Accessed December 1, 2019. https://baseballhall.org/hof/hoffman-trevor.

Net Worth Stats. "Ivan Rodriguez Net Worth." Last updated November 2019. https://www.networthstats.com/baseball-player/ivan-rodriguez-net-worth/.

Neumann, Thomas. "Ten Things to Know on the 25th Anniversary of Bo Jackson's Final NFL Game." *ESPN.com*, January 13, 2016. https://www.espn.com/nfl/story/_/id/14559718/bo-jackson-10-things-know-25th-anniversary-final-nfl-game.

New World Encyclopedia. "Mikey Mantle." Last updated October 3, 2018. https://www.newworldencyclopedia.org/entry/Mickey_Mantle.

Okrent, Daniel, and Steve Wulf. *Baseball Anecdotes.* New York: Harper Perennial, 1989; originally published by Oxford University Press.

Pennsylvania Center for the Book. "Mike Schmidt." Accessed December 1, 2019. https://pabook.libraries.psu.edu/schmidt_mike.

Pomrenke, Jacob. "Chipper Jones." *Society for American Baseball Research.* Last updated June 13, 2018. https://sabr.org/bioproj/person/b7c916e5.

Positive Coaching Alliance. "Tony La Russa." Accessed December 1, 2019. https://www.positivecoach.org/team/la-russa-tony/.

Rasbach, David. "Griffey Just 'a Kid' During His Time in Bellingham." *The Bellingham Herald.* July 18, 2016. https://www.bellinghamherald.com/sports/mlb/seattle-mariners/article90165597.html.

Reineking, Jim. "To Celebrate 35th Anniversary of Start of Cal Ripken's Streak, Here Are Some Fun Facts." *USA Today.* May 30, 2017. https://www.usatoday.com/story/sports/mlb/2017/05/30/cal-ripken-consecutive-games-streak-fascinating-facts/102281920/.

RodCarew.com. "Rod Carew's Biography." Accessed December 1, 2019. https://rodcarew.com/biography/.

Schoenfield, David. "The Best Lineups of All Time: Big Red Machine or Murderer's Row?" ESPN.com, January 19, 2016. https://www.espn.com/blog/sweetspot/post/_/id/67749/the-best-lineups-of-all-time-big-red-machine-or-murderers-row.

Shaughnessy, Dan. "Red Sox Living Legend Carl Yastrzemski Remains a Grand Figure." *The Boston Globe*. March 8, 2019. https://www.bostonglobe.com/sports/redsox/2019/03/08/red-sox-living-legend-carl-yastrzemski-remains-grand-figure/Kda3kJ9OGjxvokHOIh6jOO/story.html.

Shepard, Matthew. "Sparky Anderson: Honoring a Legend." *Bleacher Report*. April 8, 2011. https://bleacherreport.com/articles/650012-sparky-anderson-honoring-a-legend.

Siegal, Justine. "Call Me Coach." *The Players' Tribune*, December 10, 2015. https://www.theplayerstribune.com/en-us/articles/justine-siegal-mlb-coach.

Small Business Journal. "Exclusive Cal Ripken Jr. Interview. Talking Life After Baseball (The Ripken Way)." February 27, 2018. https://thesbjournal.com/featured/cal-ripken-jr-interview/.

Smith, Brian T. "Craig Biggio's Road to Cooperstown Paved with Pine Tar and Grit." *Houston Chronicle*. July 23, 2015. Updated July 26, 2015. https://www.houstonchronicle.com/sports/astros/article/Craig-Biggio-s-road-to-Cooperstown-paved-with-6401475.php.

South, John. "Willie McCovey." *Encyclopedia of Alabama*. Last updated March 6, 2019. http://www.encyclopediaofalabama.org/article/h-4078.

Sports Illustrated Kids. "Mo'ne Davis Part of TIME Firsts." September 7, 2017. https://www.sikids.com/si-kids/2017/09/07/mone-davis-part-time-firsts-project.

Stone, Larry. "Edgar Martinez's Improbable Path to Becoming a Mariners Icon." *The Seattle Times*. August 11, 2017. https://www.seattletimes.com/sports/mariners/edgar-martinezs-improbable-path-to-becoming-a-mariners-icon/.

Stone, Larry. "For Mariners fans and teammates alike, why the connection to Edgar Martinez is so deep and so emotional." *The Seattle Times*, July 19, 2019. https://www.seattletimes.com/sports/mariners/for-mariners-fans-and-teammates-alike-why-the-connection-to-edgar-martinez-is-so-deep-and-so-emotional/.

This Day in Baseball. "Reggie Jackson Biography." Accessed December 1, 2019. https://thisdayinbaseball.com/reggie-jackson-biography/.

Verducci, Tom. "The Left Arm of God: Sandy Koufax Was More Than Just a Perfect Pitcher," *Sports Illustrated*, August 29, 2014. https://www.si.com/mlb/2014/08/29/sandy-koufax-dodgers-left-arm-god-si-60.

REFERENCES

Verducci, Tom. "Once in a Lifetime." *Sports Illustrated,* August 14, 1995. https://www.si.com/vault/1995/08/14/8095773/once-in-a-lifetime -greg-maddux-of-the-braves-is-the-best-righthander-in-the-past -75-yearsbut-he-would-rather-you-didnt-know-it.

Wancho, Joseph. "Randy Johnson." *Society for American Baseball Research.* Accessed December 1, 2019. https://sabr.org/bioproj/person /e905e1ef.

Wancho, Joseph. "Rickey Henderson." *Society for American Baseball Research.* Last updated January 3, 2018. https://sabr.org/bioproj/person /957d4da0.

WBRU. "Pedro Martinez Foundation Aims To Prepare Kids In Case Baseball Dreams Don't Come True." October 26, 2018. https://www .wbur.org/hereandnow/2018/10/26/pedro-martinez-foundation -dominican-republic-baseball.

Weese, Lucas. "Willie McCovey's Legacy Will Never Be Forgotten." *Last Word on Baseball.* October 31, 2018. https://lastwordonbaseball .com/2018/10/31/willie-mccovey-never-forgotten/.

West, Steve. "Ivan Rodriguez." *Society for American Baseball Research.* Last updated January 31, 2017. https://sabr.org/bioproj/person/2eafa5bc.

West, Steve. "Wade Boggs." *Society for American Baseball Research.* Last updated April 1, 2016. https://sabr.org/bioproj/person/e083ea50.

Who2Biographies. "Mike Piazza Biography." Accessed December 1, 2019. https://www.who2.com/bio/mike-piazza/.

Will, George F. "A Head for the Game." *Sports Illustrated.* March 12, 1990. https://www.si.com/vault/issue/710889/63.

Woullard, Jason. "The Kid: Baseball's Purest Superstar." *The Shadow League.* July 25, 2014. https://theshadowleague.com/the-kid-baseball -s-purest-superstar/.

WSB. "Mariano Rivera: Lessons in Perseverance, Drive, and Building a Legendary Career from the Ground Up." Accessed December 1, 2019. https://www.wsb.com/speakers/mariano-rivera.

INDEX

A

Aaron, Hank, 111–112
Abbott, Jim, 23
Adock, Joe, 111
Alomar, Roberto, 52
Alou, Felipe, 67
Anderson, Sparky, 32, 88, 133

B

Bagwell, Jeff, 42
Banks, Ernie, 75
Bell, Derek, 42
Beltre, Adrian, 64
Bench, Johnny, 26–27, 31–32, 88
Berry, Sean, 42
Biggio, Craig, 42, 46–51
Blue, Vida, xi
Bonds, Barry, 111
Brock, Lou, 83

C

Carew, Rod, 52
Céspedes, Yoennis, 101
Chapman, Aroldis, 101
Clemente, Roberto, 110, 116
Concepción, Dave, 88

D

Darvish, Yu, 35
Davis, Charles "Chili," 121
Davis, Mo'ne, 11
DiMaggio, Joe, 42, 97

F

Finley, Charlie, 122
Fisk, Carlton, 31, 135
Foster, George, 88

G

Gehrig, Lou, 35, 42–43, 56, 70, 72–73
Gerónimo, César, 88
Gibson, Bob, 7, 41, 122
Glavine, Tom, 8–9, 19
Griffey, Ken, Jr., 90–96, 118
Griffey, Ken, Sr., 88, 92–95
Guerrero, Vladimir, 67
Gwynn, Tony, 109

H

Henderson, Rickey, 78–84
Hernández, Orlando "El Duque," 101
Hoffman, Trevor, 22–23

J

Jackson, Bo, 123–124
Jackson, Reggie, 109–110
Johnson, Randy, 6, 12–18, 107, 118
Jones, "Chipper," 58–63

K

Kinugasa, Sachio, 35
Koufax, Sandy, 20–21

L

La Russa, Tony, 126–132
Long, Dale, 96

M

Mack, Connie, 131, 133–134
Maddux, Greg, xvi–5, 8–9
Mantle, Mickey, 97
Martinez, Edgar, 95, 114–120
Martinez, Pedro, 6, 40, 67
Mathews, Eddie, 65
Matsui, Hideki, 35
Matsuzaka, Daisuke, 35
Mattingly, Don, 96
Mays, Willie, 98–99

McCovey, Willie, 41
McGraw, John, 131, 132
Mecir, Jim, 77
Molitor, Paul, 121
Morgan, Joe, 53, 88

N
Nomo, Hideo, 35

O
Oh, Sadaharu, 35
Ortiz, David, xi, 36–41, 67

P
Pérez, Tony, 88
Pettitte, Andy, 19
Piazza, Mike, 30
Pride, Curtis, 113
Puig, Yasiel, x, 101
Pujols, Albert, 67

R
Raines, Tim, 85
Rickey, Branch, 55
Ripken, Billy, 73
Ripken, Cal, Jr., ix, 43, 68–73
Ripken, Cal, Sr., 70, 72–73
Rivera, Mariano, 22–23
Robinson, Jackie, 55, 100
Rodriguez, Alex, 74

Rodríguez, Iván, 24–30
Rose, Pete, 88
Ruth, Babe, v, 34, 42, 56–57, 111
Ryan, Nolan, 6

S
Santiago, Benito, 27
Schmidt, Mike, 64
Seaver, Tom, 7–8
Siegal, Justine, 45
Smith, Ozzie, 74
Smoltz, John, 8–9
Suzuki, Ichiro, ix, 35, 102–109

T
Thomas, Frank, 125
Tiant, Luis, 101
Torre, Joe, 21, 132

V
Virgil, Osvaldo, Sr., 67
Vizquel, Omar, 74–75

W
Williams, Ted, 56, 87, 98
Woods, Tiger, 9

Y
Yastrzemski, Carl, 85

ABOUT THE AUTHOR

Dean Burrell is a decades-long baseball fan, having learned the game by watching the greats at Candlestick Park in San Francisco. He lives and works in the Bay Area. Dean is fortunate enough to have access to two local major league teams and has been known to sneak out of work to attend day games (but don't tell his boss).

NOTES

NOTES

NOTES

NOTES

NOTES

NOTES

NOTES

NOTES

NOTES